Meditation

Meditation

by

Wendi Momen

'One hour's reflection is preferable to
seventy years of pious worship.'

GEORGE RONALD
OXFORD

GEORGE RONALD, Publisher
46 High Street, Kidlington, Oxford OX5 2DN

A Cataloguing-in Publication entry
is available from the British Library

ISBN 0-85398-407-7

Typeset by Leith Editorial Services, Abingdon, UK
Printed and bound in Great Britain
by Redwood Books

Contents

To my mother

Preface

Inspired and encouraged by the advice of Shoghi Effendi that

> As we have such wonderful prayers and meditations in our writings, the reading of these with friends who are interested in and crave for this type of small meeting is often a step towards attracting them to the Faith. Perhaps you could start such an activity in your city.[1]

a group of Bahá'ís and friends began to meet fortnightly to explore different forms of meditation and relaxation, using as the focus of our meditation the Bahá'í scriptures. This book is the product of those gatherings.

1
Beginnings

In many places in the Bahá'í writings we are urged to 'meditate upon this', to 'ponder', to 'reflect'. Bahá'u'lláh affirms that 'One hour's reflection is preferable to seventy years of pious worship'[1] and Bahá'u'lláh Himself revealed a number of meditations. 'Prayerful meditation on the teachings' is one of the six 'essential requisites for our spiritual growth' summarized by the Universal House of Justice.[2] Meditation is one of the purposes of the Bahá'í fast.[3] Bahá'ís are encouraged to meditate and may even to gather to do so, as 'such a communion helps in fostering fellowship among the believers'.[4] At the same time, the Universal House of Justice has pointed out that meditation is, generally, not 'a group therapy' but rather a 'private individual activity'.[5]

We know that 'through meditation the doors of deeper knowledge and inspiration may be opened',[6] that 'the core of religious faith is that mystic feeling which unites man with God' and that 'this state of spiritual communion can be brought about and maintained by means of meditation and prayer'.[7] We learn from the Bahá'í writings that the ability to meditate 'brings forth from the invisible plane the sciences and arts', that through it 'inventions are made possible, colossal undertakings are carried out' and even that 'governments can run smoothly'.[8]

Such an important feature of life surely merits development. However, many of us do not know what meditation is or how to go about it. There are so many forms, rituals, techniques propounded by adherents of one discipline or another that we are bewildered by their variety, unsure which, if any, are consistent with the teachings of Bahá'u'lláh.

Bahá'u'lláh Himself specified no particular method, procedure or ritual practices for meditation, so Bahá'ís are 'free to do as they wish in this area'.[9] There is 'no reason' why Bahá'ís 'should not be taught to meditate, but they should guard against superstitious or foolish ideas creeping into it',[10] something that can be avoided by heeding the advice of the Guardian 'to always use and read, during your hours of meditation and prayer, the words revealed by Bahá'u'lláh and the Master'.[11]

Thus this book uses the Bahá'í scriptures as the focus for meditation while describing briefly a number of techniques and practices that one might employ to develop this faculty. We begin by looking at what meditation is, from the perspective of the Bahá'í Faith, and what is its purpose and goal. The following chapter considers concepts of meditation held by other traditions and techniques of meditation developed by them, as well as some suggestions for private or group meditation. Chapter 4 provides a number of short verses from the Bahá'í teachings, grouped into themes, that may be useful to reflect upon during meditation. Chapter 5 is a selection of the longer meditations revealed by Bahá'u'lláh, while Chapter 6 contains some of the verses upon which Bahá'u'lláh has asked us to meditate. Chapter 7 is focused on the 'great questions' that 'Abdu'l-Bahá has said meditation can answer, while the final chapter centres on the themes that the Universal House of Justice suggests will, if studied profoundly, provide a 'clearer apprehension of the purpose of God for man'.

2
What is Meditation?

Meditate profoundly, that the secret of things
unseen may be revealed unto you, that you may
inhale the sweetness of a spiritual and
imperishable fragrance, and that you may
acknowledge the truth that from time immemorial
even unto eternity the Almighty hath tried, and
will continue to try, His servants, so that light may
be distinguished from darkness, truth from
falsehood, right from wrong, guidance from error,
happiness from misery, and roses from thorns.[1]

Bahá'u'lláh

Is meditation merely 'thinking hard' about something, focusing, concentrating? Is it letting one's
mind wander about aimlessly while one is in a
dreamy, semi-conscious state? Or is it having no
thoughts at all? To meditate, according to the
Concise Oxford Dictionary, is to 'exercise the
mind in (esp. religious) contemplation'; to contemplate is to 'survey with the eyes or in the

mind'. Clearly these definitions are inadequate to describe the rich and deeply moving experience that most of us encounter – or expect to encounter – when we meditate.

In 1913, at the Friend's Meeting House in St Martin's Lane, London, 'Abdu'l-Bahá, the son of the founder of Bahá'í Faith, described the nature of meditation and its value to individuals and society.[2] He recalled a society formed in Persia about a thousand years ago, also called the Society of Friends, who 'gathered together for silent communion with the Almighty'. By 'meditating and turning their faces to the Source of Light . . . all the Divine problems were solved'. When faced with a decision to be made, they would come together in silence and, 'freeing their minds from everything else', they would 'sit and reflect'. 'Before long' the answer to the problem would be 'revealed to them'. 'Many abstruse divine questions', 'Abdu'l-Bahá affirmed, were 'solved by this illumination', including such age-old mysteries as the 'reality of the spirit of man' and life after death, as well as 'the scientific questions of the day' and even the 'the essential nature of Divinity'. Called the 'Followers of the inner light', these people attained to 'a superlative degree of power', and were 'entirely freed from blind dogmas and imitations'.

This description of meditation as seeking answers to questions while sitting in silence and 'turning to the Source of Light' is familiar to stu-

dents of many forms of meditation. As we shall
see, there are other schools of thought as to what
meditation is and what its goals are, but 'Abdu'l-
Bahá states that meditation is 'speaking with
your own spirit':

> It is an axiomatic fact that while you meditate you
> are speaking with your own spirit. In that state of
> mind you put certain questions to your spirit and
> the spirit answers: the light breaks forth and the
> reality is revealed.

The questions one puts to one's spirit do not have
to be problems requiring specific solutions but
may address the issues that have perplexed
humanity from the beginning – why are we here?
where are we going? how can we best prepare for
our journey? 'Abdu'l-Bahá says that 'Meditation
is the key for opening the doors of mysteries.'

So important is the ability to meditate that
'Abdu'l-Bahá says 'You cannot apply the name
"man" to any being void of this faculty of meditation; without it he would be a mere animal,
lower than the beasts'.

The goals of the kind of meditation described
by 'Abdu'l-Bahá are not at all superficial or temporary but are at the very heart of the purpose of
our existence:

• Through the faculty of meditation man
  attains to eternal life;

- through it he receives the breath of the Holy Spirit – the bestowal of the Spirit is given in reflection and meditation.

- The spirit of man is itself informed and strengthened during meditation;

- through it affairs of which man knew nothing are unfolded before his view.

- Through it he receives Divine inspiration,

- through it he receives heavenly food.

- This faculty of meditation frees man from the animal nature,

- discerns the reality of things,

- puts man in touch with God.

As we shall see, many traditions of meditation seek the achievement of similar, if not identical, goals.

In addition to these spiritual benefits, 'Abdu'l-Bahá describes a number of social effects to be had from meditation:

- This faculty brings forth from the invisible plane the sciences and arts.

- Through the meditative faculty inventions are made possible,

- colossal undertakings are carried out;

- through it governments can run smoothly.

However, perhaps the most significant effect of meditation is that

- Through this faculty man enters into the very Kingdom of God.

Development of the meditative faculty is, therefore, vital to the well-being and progress of both individuals and society at large. But how do we begin to develop it?

Although the Bahá'í Faith does not prescribe a formula, techniques or practices that will enable one to develop and use the faculty of meditation to the full, nevertheless 'Abdu'l-Bahá does describe some features and conditions of meditation that may be applied to reach the meditative state. The first, He says, is silence:

> Bahá'u'lláh says there is a sign (from God) in every phenomenon: the sign of the intellect is contemplation and the sign of contemplation is silence, because it is impossible for a man to do two things at one time – he cannot both speak and meditate.

The next feature of meditation is a temporary withdrawal from the world:

> In that state man abstracts himself: in that state man withdraws himself from all outside objects; in that subjective mood he is immersed in the ocean of spiritual life and can unfold the secrets of things-in-themselves.

Because 'some thoughts are useless to man; they are like waves moving in the sea without result', the faculty of meditation needs to be 'bathed in the inner light and characterized with divine attributes' in order that its 'results will be confirmed'.

The meditative capacity is, 'Abdu'l-Bahá says, like a mirror and will reflect whatever is put before it, either earthly concerns or spiritual matters. If the object of one's quest is enlightenment on a wholly material problem, perhaps a scientific enquiry, 'if the spirit of man is contemplating earthly subjects he will be informed of these'.

If, however, we are seeking spiritual enlightenment, then we are to 'turn the mirror' of our spirits 'heavenwards', so that 'the heavenly constellations and the rays of the Sun of Reality will be reflected in your hearts, and the virtues of the Kingdom will be obtained'.

'Abdu'l-Bahá urges us to focus on the spiritual dimension, suggesting that the benefits to us per-

sonally and to society as a whole can be best
achieved by directing our attention to the 'heavenly Sun', the divine kingdom:

> Therefore let us keep this faculty rightly directed –
> turning it to the heavenly Sun and not to earthly
> objects – so that we may discover the secrets of the
> Kingdom, and comprehend the allegories of the
> Bible and the mysteries of the spirit.
>
> May we indeed become mirrors reflecting the
> heavenly realities, and may we become so pure as
> to reflect the stars of heaven.

Learning to fulfil these conditions may, in itself,
pose challenges for those who have never
attempted to meditate and it is here that some of
the techniques of relaxation and meditation pro-
posed by various traditions may be useful.

> When, however, thou dost contemplate the
> innermost essence of all things, and the
> individuality of each, thou wilt behold the signs of
> thy Lord's mercy in every created thing, and see the
> spreading rays of His Names and Attributes
> throughout all the realm of being, with evidences
> which none will deny save the froward and the
> unaware. Then wilt thou observe that the universe
> is a scroll that discloseth His hidden secrets, which
> are preserved in the well-guarded Tablet. And not
> an atom of all the atoms in existence, not a
> creature from amongst the creatures but speaketh

His praise and telleth of His attributes and names, revealeth the glory of His might and guideth to His oneness and His mercy: and none will gainsay this who hath ears to hear, eyes to see, and a mind that is sound.[3]

3
Meditation Techniques

The practice of meditation is very ancient and can be found in many faith traditions. This chapter looks only briefly at a few techniques of meditation popular in the West.

It should be stressed that most techniques of meditation are parts of complex belief systems or philosophies of life, the outward expression of which are sets of rituals, movements, breathing exercises or repetitions of verses. Generally, these are considered ways of achieving the goals of the belief system, of attaining the meditative state or of assisting meditation. Hence what follows is merely an overview of these outward forms and not a description of these systems.

Some of the meditation practices described may appear to differ from the goals set out by the Bahá'í Faith but the actual exercises may in themselves be useful, even if one does not wish to accept the philosophy of the belief system in which it developed.

Practitioners of these forms will find this survey superficial in the extreme but our present purpose is to take advantage of the techniques themselves rather than to examine or adopt the belief systems. Those who are interested in pursuing the meditation paths outlined here will find a number of books, articles and classes available.

Goals of Meditation

The goals or purposes of meditation differ from tradition to tradition. For some, meditation is a way of realizing, or actualizing, one's true nature. For others, the purpose of meditation is to achieve a sense of unity with the universe or a higher sense of one's place in it. Others meditate to attain 'enlightenment' or 'illumination'; for some, this enlightenment comes from within oneself while others believe it to be external to the person, stemming from the divine or perhaps the universe itself. Some seek 'the light within', the spark of the divine in man. Others seek spiritual ecstasy or 'rapturous love'. As we have seen, 'Abdu'l-Bahá suggests that one goal of meditation is to achieve that 'mystic feeling which unites man with God', a 'state of spiritual communion'.[1]

Sufism

'The object of Sufi spiritual teaching can be expressed as: to help to refine the individual's consciousness so that it may reach the Radiances of Truth, from which one is cut off by ordinary activities of the world.'² Sufis desire to reduce the effect of the 'material attributes' that 'stand in the way of higher understanding'.³ Phrases such as 'polishing the mirror' and 'removing the dust' refer to the processes of 'liberation from those elements'.⁴

A fundamental teaching of the Sufis is _dhikr'u'lláh_, the invocation or 'remembrance' of God. The principal spiritual exercise or discipline of the Sufis is _dhikr_, the 'repetitive recitation of divine Names or short, sacred formulae, often derived from scripture'.⁵ It is 'a form of concentrative or ideational meditation in which the _dhákir_ (he who remembers) repeats over and over – either aloud or in silence – a divine name or short phrase, often to a specific breathing rhythm and while sitting in a prescribed posture.'⁶ This is different from meditation or reflection (_fikr_), during which the Sufi 'concentrating upon a religious subject, meditates according to a certain progression of ideas or a series of evocations which he assimilates and experiences'.⁷ There are many forms of Sufism and various schools with different teachings on _dhikr_. Generally, however, _dhikr_ is 'an effort to consciously unveil the spiritual nature of the soul within its proper domain' whose goal is 'the realization of God's presence within the inmost being of man'.⁸ The mechanical recitation of verses without aspiring to this goal is deemed worthless.

To practice *dhikr*, 'sit alone in some corner'[9] in a comfortable position with eyes and mouth closed. Observe the exhalation and inhalation of breath, considered negation and affirmation. The *dhákir* then recites the Muslim profession of faith, 'There is no God but God' (lá iláha illá'lláh), in two stages: the verse of negation 'There is no God' (lá iláha) while breathing out and the verse of affirmation 'but God' (illá'lláh) while breathing in. If this is continued, 'at last he will reach a state when the motion of his tongue will cease, and it will seem as though the world flowed from it'.[10] This is the stage of 'remembrance of the tongue'. 'Let him persevere in this until all trace of motion is removed from his tongue, and he finds his heart persevering in the thought.'[11] This stage is 'remembrance of the heart'. Should one continue 'until the form of the word, its letters and shape, is removed from his heart, and there remains the idea alone',[12] one has achieved 'remembrance of the inmost being'. These latter stages are very difficult to attain. The aim of *dhikr* is 'to bring about an unveiling of our spiritual self. It is the act of polishing the heart in order to make it a perfect mirror reflecting the light of God'.[13] Some Sufis practise *dhikr* for hours, even days, at a time.

Transcendental Meditation (TM)

In Transcendental Meditation the goal is to experience 'quieter and quieter levels of thinking' until one 'arrives at a state of complete mental stillness. In this state the attention is said to have gone beyond, or transcended, the everyday levels of thought . . .'[14] Specially chosen mantras are used to assist meditators to achieve this. In TM, a mantra is a meaningless word with specific qualities which 'resonate with the nervous system in a soothing harmonious manner'.[15] Practitioners use the mantra for twenty minutes twice a day. The mantra is not chanted or continually recited, either verbally or mentally; rather, one has a 'passive awareness' of it which is 'non-directed'.[16] Essentially, one mentally repeats a word while sitting still, without moving the lips or tongue. 'The mantra is not so much an object for the attention to be focused on as a vehicle on which the attention rests and which leads it down to the subtler levels of thinking.'[17] The eyes should be closed and one's attention turned inward. If the mind wanders, the mantra should be reintroduced.

Yoga

Yoga is both an 'end-goal' and a 'system of techniques and disciplines to reach the end-goal'.[18] There are many branches of Yoga and several systems, dealing with postures, breath controls and relaxation exercises. Here we are concerned with the Yoga of meditation. Many people who practice Yoga are not involved with its religious roots in Hinduism but are interested only in its physical and psychical aspects to enhance their quality of life.

The supreme goal of Yoga is 'the union of the individual spirit with the universal spirit, the finding of one's essential nature (Self) beyond empirical ego, which has to be dissolved, and the seeing and experiencing of the ground of one's being'.[19] A number of meditative methods, both active and passive, are employed to achieve this. 'Meditation' here refers to the methods of 'steadying, quieting, or opening the mind for purposes of altering states of consciousness', although it is also used for relaxation and 'mental hygiene'.[20]

An important prerequisite for meditation is a 'poised and stable sitting posture'.[21] A cushion on the floor of a pleasant, clean room, airy and neither too warm nor too cool, away from draughts and likely to be free from interruptions, is recommended. Clothing should be comfortable and light, with anything that constricts – a tie or belt – as well as shoes and stockings removed. The body, or at least the hands and face, should be washed or sponged before meditation, and the teeth brushed.

There are several postures one can adopt for meditation, the most famous being the Lotus.

However, as this can take a long time to master, other poses may be used. 'The essential factors are to sit keeping the back upright and to have the head and neck poised in line with the spine . . . In the main traditional postures the legs are crossed in some manner. The easiest Yoga posture is Easy Posture in which the legs are crossed tailor's fashion and the knees are kept as low as is comfortable.'[22] If this is difficult, the Egyptian posture can be used – sitting in a straight-backed chair with the feet and knees together, the feet flat on the ground with the palms of the hands resting on the tops of the thighs. Lying on the back is not recommended.

The purpose of adopting a meditative posture is so that the meditator can 'forget about the body and give his whole attention to quieting the mind'.[23]

There are several techniques of 'concentrative meditation', all preceded by sense-withdrawal. 'As a tortoise might withdraw its head into its shell, so you pull in the attention from external sense objects.'[24] The attention is then fixed on one thing, the meditation-object. The object of attention is not important. If the mind wanders from the meditation-object, it should be gently brought back. The ability to do this increases with practice. In this state one should be completely relaxed and serene – no clenched fists, facial expressions or hunched shoulders.

One form of concentration is 'steady gaze meditation'. Here one looks steadily at an object, blinking as necessary. When the eyes are tired they may be closed, holding the object in the mind's eye. The object may be anything, but a small object, or a small part of a larger one, is preferred. Sometimes a lighted candle in a darkened room is used, as light is often associated with mystical enlightenment, eyes are drawn to a bright point and the image of the flame is easily retained when the eyes are closed.[25] The object should be level with the eyes or a little below. Sitting in a meditative posture, one should look at the object 'in a calm, relaxed manner' but not stare at it.[26] If the mind wanders, bring it gently back to the object.

Another form of concentration is 'breathing meditation'. Sitting in a meditative posture, choose a point on which to fix the attention. This is usually 'the point in the nose where incoming air first strikes or a point a little below the navel'.[27] Breathe deeply into the abdomen through the nostrils and then out, again through the nostrils. It is not necessary to fill the lungs fully. Eventually the breathing can be left to take care of itself. During meditation 'the respiration will become slower, smoother, more rhythmic'.[28] It is recommended that beginners count each breath they take, from one to ten, and then starting over. After a month of practice, the counting can stop.

Some Yogas use *japa* as the basis for meditation. *Japa* is 'repetition of a letter, syllable, word, phrase, sentence, or sound considered to possess magical, occult, spiritual, or mystical potency and called a *mantra*'. *Mantras* are 'incantatory and mystical sounds' which may be said aloud and thought inwardly. A voiced *mantra* may be repeated thousands of times and should be said in a voice that is 'alive and resonant'. The aim is to 'utilize the power of sound vibrations to influence modalities of consciousness'.[29] Certain words are said to be particularly powerful; OM, the 'word of glory' representing the Absolute, is considered the most potent. Other *mantras* are usually Sanskrit letters, words or sentences, often preceded by OM. *Japa* can be performed in a number of ways and using a number of methods: daily, usually morning and evening; while seated; an inward repetition without the lips moving, while standing, sitting, walking or undertaking some activity; repeated aloud; whispered; repeated mentally; with the meaning of the mantra held in the mind but not voiced in any way.

There are a number of other forms of Yoga meditation, far too many to consider here. Various yoga techniques and forms are taught in schools and classes in many cities and those interested are encouraged to seek these out.

Zen

Zen is a form of Buddhism which provides a

practical method of 'realizing' the 'Buddha nature'. It is a discipline of the body and mind that 'requires great effort, perseverance and faith in both the possibility of Enlightenment and in one's own ability to attain it'.[30] The aim is 'to lead the practitioner to a direct experience of life in itself' and to eliminate 'all dualistic distinctions such as I/You, true/false, subject/object'.[31] 'The goal of Zen is Enlightenment and ever-deepening Enlightenment.'[32]

There are many forms of Zen and several schools, each with its own set of practices and emphases. However, the core of all schools of Zen is *za-zen* or seated meditation.

The place chosen for meditation should be a clean, quiet spot where one will not be disturbed. The same place should be used every time, if possible. Some use incense or put flowers on a small altar, although this is not necessary. The room should be a comfortable temperature and natural lighting is preferred.

Clothing should be loose and dark, preferably black. Clothes should be clean and fresh. A firm cushion placed on a folded blanket is used for sitting on the floor.

It is recommended that meditation is practised at a regular time or times every day. Morning is preferred if only one session can be arranged, with a second sitting before retiring to bed. Each session should last about fifteen minutes to begin with, building up to thirty minutes to an hour.

There are several postures to choose from but in all the 'ideal is to sit so that the body is perfectly upright and a vertical line can be drawn from the centre of your forehead, nose, chin, throat and navel. This is achieved by pushing the waist forward and the abdomen out.'[33] The eyes should be only half opened and focused about three to six feet away.

In the first position one sits on a chair that allows the feet to rest firmly on the ground. The back should be straight, the shoulders down and the head upright. The hands should rest in the lap, right hand under left, palms turned up with the thumbs touching at the tips forming a parallel line with the fingers.

In the second position, one kneels, straddling the cushion on the floor, and sitting back on the heels. The head, shoulders and hands are held as in position one.

In the Burmese position the legs are crossed with both feet flat on the floor and the knees touching the blanket. This can be achieved by sitting on the front half of the cushion or by adding a second cushion if necessary. If the knees will not touch the ground, put small cushions under them. The head, shoulders and hands are held as in the first position.

The half-lotus is more difficult. The left foot is put under the right thigh and the right foot under the left thigh, or vice versa. Use alternate leg positions each time.

In the lotus position ones rests each foot on the opposite thigh. It is extremely difficult to achieve but produces the greatest stability for sitting.

After choosing a suitable posture, focus attention by counting breaths, counting one for in-breaths and two for out. Do not control the breathing but let it come naturally. Should the mind wander or be distracted by thought, begin counting again once the situation is realized. If ten is reached without interference, or one inadvertently counts beyond ten, return to one and start over. Once this is mastered, only the in- or out-breaths need be counted.

When thoughts arise during meditation, they should merely be observed and allowed to pass; do not try to suppress them but neither should they be followed. It is also important to try to let go of intentional thoughts.

Chanting usually follows a period of *za-zen*. A wooden drum is beaten and a gong struck to accompany the chanting. There are a number of Zen chants, many of which repeat certain phrases or verses.

The purpose of za-zen is described by Mumon Yamadas Roshi:

> To find the jewel, one must calm the waves; it is hard to find if one stirs up the water. Where the waters of mediation are clear and calm, the mind-jewel will be naturally visible.'[34]

Relaxation

Although not in themselves meditation, the techniques used to achieve a relaxed body and mind
are widely employed to attain meditative states.
There are numerous methods of relaxation but
many have characteristics in common. Relaxation is often guided by another person, who
talks through the various stages and enables the
one practising relaxation to be passive. A variety
of relaxation tapes and recordings are available
and often use this technique.

Choose a warm, quiet location at a time of day
one is unlikely to be disturbed. Allow enough
time for session; one should not be rushed. Dis-
connect the telephone and hang a 'do not
disturb' sign on the door if necessary. Clothing
should be loose and not restrict the body. Remove
shoes, belts, ties and jangling jewellery. As one
feels the cold more when one is immobile for any
length of time, a blanket to cover or wrap around
oneself is useful.

If the room is darkened, some people like to
burn candles to create a pleasant atmosphere.
Some burn incense or aromatic oils. Some people
prefer complete silence, others use recorded
music – often 'new-age' music without melody
or rhythm – or sounds from nature – ocean
waves, wind in trees – as a background.

Generally, one should assume a comfortable
position in which every muscle of the body can
eventually relax. Many find that lying on one's

back on the floor or a firm bed is most suitable. A small cushion tucked under the knees to keep them slightly bent, and thereby relaxing the leg, is useful.

Breathing is natural but each breath is observed or 'followed'. As one focuses on breathing, each muscle of the body is relaxed in turn, usually starting with the feet and ankles and working up the body. Images such as the body part getting heavy and sinking into the floor, 'putting down roots' or, alternatively, becoming light and floating, assist in this process.

When the body is fully relaxed, the mind is also helped to relax and rid itself of 'busyness'. In guided relaxation one is often asked to imagine oneself wandering in a garden or up a hill or along a path. One is asked to take note of the shape, colour and fragrance of the flowers, the texture of the grass on the hill, the noise of the pebbles as one walks along the path, all the while keeping the muscles relaxed. Simple phrases, affirmations or 'truth statements' may be introduced which enable one to focus on a particular thought or idea.

At the end of the relaxation session one is slowly brought back to 'life'. One walks down the hill or back along the path; the roots are drawn in. One by one parts of the body are slowly moved and gradually one is able to sit or stand up.

Relaxation techniques are widely used to

reduce stress and anxiety and to provide an oasis of calm, peace and beauty in a busy day.

From the Bahá'í Writings

Whilst it is the case that no form of meditation is prescribed for Bahá'ís, some aspects of the techniques used in the different meditation traditions and the goals they aim to achieve can be found in the Bahá'í writings.

For example, Bahá'ís will be familiar with the Sufi concept of 'polishing the mirror' of the heart so as better to reflect the attributes of God and of the effort required to do this:

> From the exalted source, and out of the essence of His favour and bounty He hath entrusted every created thing with a sign of His knowledge, so that none of His creatures may be deprived of its share in expressing, each according to its capacity and rank, this knowledge. This sign is the mirror of His beauty in the world of creation. The greater the effort exerted for the refinement of this sublime and noble mirror, the more faithfully will it be made to reflect the glory of the names and attributes of God, and reveal the wonders of His signs and knowledge. Every created thing will be enabled (so great is this reflecting power) to reveal the potentialities of its pre-ordained station, will recognize its capacity and limitations, and will testify to the truth that 'He, verily, is God; there is

none other God besides Him' . . .

There can be no doubt whatever that, in consequence of the efforts which every man may consciously exert and as a result of the exertion of his own spiritual faculties, this mirror can be so cleansed from the dross of earthly defilements and purged from satanic fancies as to be able to draw nigh unto the meads of eternal holiness and attain the courts of everlasting fellowship.[35]

However, whereas the Sufi believes that this can be achieved by one's own efforts, Bahá'u'lláh states that the Manifestations of God are needed to assist the process:

Upon the reality of man . . . He hath focused the radiance of all of His names and attributes, and made it a mirror of His own Self . . .

These energies with which the Day Star of Divine bounty and Source of heavenly guidance hath endowed the reality of man lie, however, latent within him, even as the flame is hidden within the candle and the rays of light are potentially present in the lamp. The radiance of these energies may be obscured by worldly desires even as the light of the sun can be concealed beneath the dust and dross which cover the mirror. Neither the candle nor the lamp can be lighted through their own unaided efforts, nor can it ever be possible for the mirror to free itself from its dross. It is clear and evident that until a fire is kindled the lamp will never be ignited,

and unless the dross is blotted out from the face of
the mirror it can never represent the image of the
sun nor reflect its light and glory.

And since there can be no tie of direct
intercourse to bind the one true God with His
creation, and no resemblance whatever can exist
between the transient and the Eternal, the
contingent and the Absolute, He hath ordained
that in every age and dispensation a pure and
stainless Soul be made manifest in the kingdoms of
earth and heaven. Unto this subtle, this mysterious
and ethereal Being He hath assigned a twofold
nature; the physical, pertaining to the world of
matter, and the spiritual, which is born of the
substance of God Himself . . .

. . . Led by the light of unfailing guidance, and
invested with supreme sovereignty, They are
commissioned to use the inspiration of Their
words, the effusions of Their infallible grace and
the sanctifying breeze of Their Revelation for the
cleansing of every longing heart and receptive
spirit from the dross and dust of earthly cares and
limitations. Then, and only then, will the Trust of
God, latent in the reality of man, emerge, as
resplendent as the rising Orb of Divine Revelation,
from behind the veil of concealment, and implant
the ensign of its revealed glory upon the summits
of men's hearts.[36]

A form of the practice of _dhikr_, which Sufis use
to achieve this polish, can also be found in the

Bahá'í writings. Indeed, the daily repetition of the Greatest Name ninety-five times after the ritual washing of ones hands and face and while sitting 'turned unto God' can be seen in this light:

> It hath been ordained that every believer in God, the Lord of Judgement, shall, each day, having washed his hands and then his face, seat himself and, turning unto God, repeat 'Alláh-u-Abhá' ninety-five times.[37]

The Sufi concept of _dhikr'u'lláh_, the remembrance of God, is also found in the writings of Bahá'u'lláh:

> True remembrance is to make mention of the Lord, the All-Praised, and forget aught else beside Him.[38]

The practice of _dhikr_ and _dhikr'u'lláh_ are linked in many of the Bahá'í writings:

> Happy the days that have been consecrated to the remembrance of God, and blessed the hours which have been spent in praise of Him Who is the All-Wise.[39]

The stages of _dhikr_ – 'remembrance of the tongue', 'remembrance of the heart' and 'remembrance of the inmost being' – are also mentioned in the writings of Bahá'u'lláh:

> Cleanse from your hearts the love of worldly
> things, from your tongues every remembrance
> except His remembrance, from your entire being
> whatsoever may deter you from beholding His
> face, or may tempt you to follow the promptings of
> your evil and corrupt inclinations. Let God be your
> fear, O people, and be ye of them that tread the
> path of righteousness.[40]

The purpose of _dhikr_, polishing the mirror of
the heart from all defilement, is mentioned
several times in the Bahá'í writings:

> Say: Deliver your souls, O people, from the
> bondage of self, and purify them from all
> attachment to anything besides Me. Remembrance
> of Me cleanseth all things from defilement, could
> ye but perceive it. Say: Were all created things to be
> entirely divested of the veil of worldly vanity and
> desire, the Hand of God would in this Day clothe
> them, one and all, with the robe 'He doeth
> whatsoever He willeth in the kingdom of creation',
> that thereby the sign of His sovereignty might be
> manifested in all things. Exalted then be He, the
> Sovereign Lord of all, the Almighty, the Supreme
> Protector, the All-Glorious, the Most Powerful.
>   Intone, O My servant, the verses of God that
> have been received by thee, as intoned by them who
> have drawn nigh unto Him, that the sweetness of
> thy melody may kindle thine own soul, and attract
> the hearts of all men. Whoso reciteth, in the

privacy of his chamber, the verses revealed by God, the scattering angels of the Almighty shall scatter abroad the fragrance of the words uttered by his mouth, and shall cause the heart of every righteous man to throb. Though he may, at first, remain unaware of its effect, yet the virtue of the grace vouchsafed unto him must needs sooner or later exercise its influence upon his soul. Thus have the mysteries of the Revelation of God been decreed by virtue of the Will of Him Who is the Source of power and wisdom.[41]

The state in which one is so imbued with the remembrance of God and His verses that one is constantly, almost unconsciously, aware of them, is also spoken of by Bahá'u'lláh:

> . . . He [the Báb] said: 'Bid them recite: "Is there any Remover of difficulties save God? Say: Praised be God! He is God! All are His servants, and all abide by His bidding!" Tell them to repeat it five hundred times, nay, a thousand times, by day and by night, sleeping and waking, that haply the Countenance of Glory may be unveiled to their eyes, and tiers of light descend upon them.' He Himself, I was subsequently informed, recited this same verse, His face betraying the utmost sadness.[42]

As in Sufi practice, Bahá'u'lláh suggests that the mere repetition of words is not sufficient to attain the objective of _dhikr_ to 'consciously unveil the spiritual nature of the soul':

> Cause me to taste, O my Lord, the divine sweetness of Thy remembrance and praise. I swear by Thy might! Whosoever tasteth of its sweetness will rid himself of all attachment to the world and all that is therein, and will set his face towards Thee, cleansed from the remembrance of any one except Thee.
>
> Inspire then my soul, O my God, with Thy wondrous remembrance, that I may glorify Thy name. Number me not with them who read Thy words and fail to find Thy hidden gift which, as decreed by Thee, is contained therein, and which quickeneth the souls of Thy creatures and the hearts of Thy servants.[43]

The goal of _dhikr_, 'the realization of God's presence within the inmost being of man', is also identified in the Bahá'í writings. Many of the Hidden Words point to God's 'presence' within us:

> Turn thy sight unto thyself, that thou mayest find Me standing within thee, mighty, powerful and self-subsisting.[44]

> O Son of Man! If thou lovest Me, turn away from thyself; and if thou seekest My pleasure, regard not thine own; that thou mayest die in Me and I may eternally live in thee.[45]

O Son of Being! With the hands of power I made
thee and with the fingers of strength I created thee;
and within thee have I placed the essence of My
light.[46]

O Son Being! Thou art My lamp and My light is in
thee.[47]

Attaining the presence of God is a goal of Sufis
and many others. Indeed, it is the very purpose of
our creation:

The purpose of God in creating man hath been,
and will ever be, to enable him to know his Creator
and to attain His Presence.[48]

Blessed are they that have attained His presence.[49]

Meditating on the word of God can assist one to
His presence:

Ponder a while upon the verses concerning the
Divine Presence, which have been sent down in the
Qur'án by Him Who is the Lord of the kingdom of
names, perchance thou mayest discover the
Straight Path. . .[50]

The quieting of the soul or mind is another
typical objective of meditation in many traditions, including Sufism, Transcendental Meditation, Yoga and Zen. Bahá'u'lláh suggests that the

Sufi concept of _dhikr'u'lláh_, the remembrance of God, coupled with _dhikr_, here a recounting of God's glory, will 'quiet the heart' and create gladness:

> By Thy glory, O my God! Though I recognize and firmly believe that no description which any except Thyself can give of Thee can beseem Thy grandeur, and that no glory ascribed to Thee by any save Thyself can ever ascend into the atmosphere of Thy presence, yet were I to hold my peace, and cease to glorify Thee and to recount Thy wondrous glory, my heart would be consumed, and my soul would melt away.
>
> My remembrance of Thee, O my God, quencheth my thirst, and quieteth my heart. My soul delighteth in its communion with Thee, as the sucking child delighteth itself in the breasts of Thy mercy; and my heart panteth after Thee even as one sore athirst panteth after the living waters of Thy bounty, O Thou Who art the God of mercy, in Whose hand is the lordship of all things!
>
> I give thanks to Thee, O my God, that Thou hast suffered me to remember Thee. What else but remembrance of Thee can give delight to my soul or gladness to my heart?[51]

In this passage we also find the 'panting' of the heart, recalling the 'hammering' of the heartbeat when the recitation of verses is aligned with it in _dhikr_.[52]

Other practices found in the various traditions of meditation are also parallelled in some of the Bahá'í writings. For example, several traditions, such as Yoga, recommend that one meditate in the morning and evening. Bahá'ís are to 'recite . . . the verses of God every morn and eventide':

> Recite ye the verses of God every morn and eventide. Whoso faileth to recite them hath not been faithful to the Covenant of God and His Testament . . . Pride not yourselves on much reading of the verses or on a multitude of pious acts by night and day; for were a man to read a single verse with joy and radiance it would be better for him than to read with lassitude all the Holy Books of God, the Help in Peril, the Self-Subsisting. Read ye the sacred verses in such measure that ye be not overcome by languor and despondence. Lay not upon your souls that which will weary them and weigh them down, but rather what will lighten and uplift them, so that they may soar on the wings of Divine verses towards the Dawning-place of His manifest signs; this will draw you nearer to God, did ye but comprehend.[53]

In contrast to some techniques of meditation, here Bahá'u'lláh points out the futility, even harm, of certain practices, such as the recitation of verses over many hours or days, indicating that the purpose should be to 'lighten and uplift' the soul, not weary it.

In some meditation traditions verses are voiced aloud. For example, those who practice japa, the repetition of words or verses, are to use a voice that is 'alive and resonant', the aim being to 'utilize the power of sound vibrations to influence modalities of consciousness'. In the writings of Bahá'u'lláh we find that the use of a 'melodious' voice in recitation will enable one to appreciate the different 'worlds of God':

> They who recite the verses of the All-Merciful in the most melodious tones will perceive in them that which the sovereignty of earth and heaven can never be compared. From them they will inhale the divine fragrance of My worlds – worlds which today none can discern save those who have been endowed with vision through this sublime, this beauteous Revelation. Say: These verses draw hearts that are pure unto those spiritual worlds that can neither be expressed in worlds not intimated by allusion.[54]

In many traditions the goal of meditation is communion with God. Bahá'u'lláh Himself suggests that we should seek this:

> O Son of Light! Forget all save Me and commune with My spirit. This is of the essence of My command, therefore turn unto it.[55]

Zen Buddhists and those who practise Yoga use

meditation as a way to seek and gain enlightenment. This is a worthy goal, described in this
prayer and benediction of Bahá'u'lláh:

> Cleanse me with the waters of Thy mercy, O my
> Lord, and make me wholly Thine, and cause me to
> approach the Tabernacle of Thy Cause and the
> adored Sanctuary of Thy Presence. Ordain, then,
> for me all the things Thou didst ordain for the
> chosen ones among Thy handmaidens, and rain
> down upon me that which will illuminate my face
> and enlighten my heart.[56]

> Blessed the man who hath sought enlightenment
> from the Day-Star of My Word.[57]

Bahá'u'lláh suggests that enlightenment comes
from a knowledge of God:

> Illumine our eyes, O my Lord, with the effulgence
> of Thy beauty, and enlighten our hearts with the
> splendours of Thy knowledge and wisdom.[58]

> Set, then, our feet firm, O my God, in Thy Cause,
> and enlighten our hearts with the effulgence of
> Thy knowledge, and illumine our breasts with the
> brightness of Thy names.[59]

'Abdu'l-Bahá states that the Manifestations of
God, the source of the knowledge of God, bring
enlightenment:

God sent His Prophets into the world to teach and
enlighten man, to explain to him the mystery of
the Power of the Holy Spirit, to enable him to
reflect the light, and so in his turn, to be the source
of guidance to others.[60]

Enlightenment is to be sought from God only,
through the teachings of His Manifestations:

O Son of Spirit! I created thee rich, why dost thou
bring thyself down to poverty? Noble I made thee,
wherewith dost thou abase thyself? Out of the
essence of knowledge I gave thee being, why
seekest thou enlightenment from anyone beside
Me?[61]

Meditating on certain concepts and verses will
produce enlightenment:

O people of God! In this day everyone should fix
his eyes upon the horizon of these blessed words:
'Alone and unaided He doeth whatsoever He
pleaseth.' Whoso attaineth this station hath verily
attained the light of the essential unity of God and
is enlightened thereby . . .[62]

'Abdu'l-Bahá described the qualifications of the
enlightened soul:

As to the seven qualifications (of the divinely
enlightened soul) of which thou hast asked an

explanation, it is as follows:

Knowledge. Man must attain the knowledge of God.

Faith.

Steadfastness.

Truthfulness. Truthfulness is the foundation of all the virtues of the world of humanity. Without truthfulness, progress and success in all of the worlds of God are impossible for a soul.

When this holy attribute is established in man, all the divine qualities will also become realized.

Uprightness. And this is one of the greatest divine attainments.

Fidelity. This is also a beautiful trait of the heavenly man.

Evanescence or Humility. That is to say, man must become evanescent in God. Must forget his own selfish conditions that he may thus arise to the station of sacrifice. It should be to such a degree that if he sleep, it should not be for pleasure, but to rest the body in order to do better, to speak better, to explain more beautifully, to serve the servants of God and to prove the truths. When he remains awake, he should seek to be attentive, serve the Cause of God and sacrifice his own stations for those of God. When he attains to this station, the confirmations of the Holy Spirit will surely reach him, and man with this power can withstand all who inhabit the earth.[63]

The objective of many meditation techniques is

to achieve a state of ecstacy or spiritual rapture, often described as a 'burning desire', 'fire' or 'flame' of love. The Bahá'í writings describe a similar goal:

Ignite, then, O my God, within my breast the fire of Thy love, that its flame may burn up all else except my remembrance of Thee, that every trace of corrupt desire may be entirely mortified within me, and that naught may remain except the glorification of Thy transcendent and all-glorious Being. This is my highest aspiration, mine ardent desire, O Thou Who rulest all things, and in Whose hand is the kingdom of the entire creation.[64]

All praise be to Thee, O Lord, my God! How mysterious the Fire which Thou hast enkindled within my heart! My very limbs testify to the intensity of its heat, and evince the consuming power of its flame.[65]

O Son of Worldliness! Pleasant is the realm of being, wert thou to attain thereto; glorious is the domain of eternity, shouldst thou pass beyond the world of mortality; sweet is the holy ecstasy if thou drinkest of the mystic chalice from the hands of the celestial Youth. Shouldst thou attain this station, thou wouldst be freed from destruction and death, from toil and sin.[66]

O My servants! Deprive not yourselves of the unfading and resplendent Light that shineth within the Lamp of Divine glory. Let the flame of the love of God burn brightly within your radiant hearts. Feed it with the oil of Divine guidance, and protect it within the shelter of your constancy. Guard it within the globe of trust and detachment from all else but God, so that the evil whisperings of the ungodly may not extinguish its light.[67]

Ignite, then, within their hearts the torch of Thy love, that its flame may consume all else except their wondrous remembrance of Thee, and that no trace may be left in those hearts except the gem-like evidences of Thy most holy sovereignty . . .[68]

The aspiration of many who meditate is unity with the cosmos, 'the union of the individual spirit with the universal spirit', as in Yoga, or 'to attain the presence of God through meditation and prayer, contemplation and ecstacy',[69] as in Sufism. While Bahá'ís do not accept that the human can ever become one with God, there is a state described by Bahá'u'lláh in *The Seven Valleys* of such close communion with God that a person 'lives in God':

After scaling the high summits of wonderment the wayfarer cometh to the Valley of True Poverty and Absolute Nothingness.

This station is the dying from self and the living
in God, the being poor in self and rich in the
Desired One. Poverty as here referred to signifieth
being poor in the things of the created world, rich
in the things of God's world. For when the true
lover and devoted friend reacheth to the presence
of the Beloved, the sparkling beauty of the Loved
One and the fire of the lover's heart will kindle a
blaze and burn away all veils and wrappings. Yea,
all he hath, from heart to skin, will be set aflame,
so that nothing will remain save the Friend.[70]

The Seven Valleys is, of course, a response to
questions posed by a student of Sufism, and
describes the stages of the progress of the soul.

Many of the meditation systems require that
one reflect on one's own doings as a contrast to
the behaviour to which one can aspire. Bahá'u'l-
láh also recommends this practice:

O Son of Being! Bring thyself to account each day
ere thou art summoned to a reckoning; for death,
unheralded, shall come upon thee and thou shalt
be called to give account for thy deeds.[71]

The traditions of meditation outlined above
describe various postures useful for attaining the
meditative state. As we have seen, Bahá'u'lláh
states in the Kitáb-i-Aqdas that the repetition of
Alláh-u-Abhá ninety-five times is to be done
while seated.[72] The long and medium obligatory

prayers require a number of postures: standing, standing turned towards God (the Qiblih), standing with hands upraised, sitting, kneeling with the forehead on the ground, bending with hands resting on the knees. The short obligatory prayer is to be offered while standing 'in an attitude of humble reverence'.[73] If an obligatory prayer is missed, a prostration is to be offered in place of each one missed, after which one sits to read the designated verse.[74] The sitting posture to be adopted is 'haykalu't-tawḥíd', the 'posture of unity', traditionally signifying a 'cross-legged position'.[75] This is the posture adopted by the Sufis for their meditations. The purpose of these postures has been noted by Shoghi Effendi:

> Shoghi Effendi explains that the few simple directions given by Bahá'u'lláh for the recital of certain prayers not only have a spiritual significance but that they also help the individual 'to fully concentrate when praying and meditating'.[76]

> 'Another traditional posture of Islam referred to in the Bahá'í writings is *qu'ud* (literally, sitting), which is identical to the "sitting on one's heel" posture of Zen Buddhism.'[77]

These few examples from the writings of Bahá'u'lláh demonstrate how many of the ideas and practices found in the meditation techniques

of other traditions are revived and given fresh
meaning in the Bahá'í Faith.

Some schools of Yoga teach the practice of
fixing one's attention on an object, the 'meditation-object'. Certain forms of Yoga practise
steadily 'gazing', or staring, at an object as a way
of heightening spiritual awareness. The writings
of Bahá'u'lláh suggest that the object on which
one should fix one's gaze is the Revelation itself:

> It behoveth every man to blot out the trace of every
> idle word from the tablet of his heart, and to gaze,
> with an open and unbiased mind, on the signs of
> His Revelation, the proofs of His Mission, and the
> tokens of His glory.[78]

However, Shoghi Effendi advised:

> If you find you need to visualize someone when you
> pray, think of the Master. Through Him you can
> address Bahá'u'lláh. Gradually try to think of the
> qualities of the Manifestation, and in that way a
> mental form will fade out, for after all the body is
> not the thing, His Spirit is there and is the essential,
> everlasting element.[79]

Suggestions for Meditation

Realizing the benefits of meditation and the effi-
cacy of some of the methods found both in the
Bahá'í teachings and in other traditions, inspires

one to begin regular meditation. Below are a few suggestions on how one might employ some of the techniques discussed in tandem with the word of God. It is stressed that these are merely suggestions and are not prescriptive. As the Universal House of Justice pointed out, 'while they may appeal to some people, they may repel others'.[80]

Recitation of Verses

As we have seen, the recitation of 'Alláh-u-Abhá' ninety-five times is prescribed by Bahá'u'lláh. The Universal House of Justice has suggested that this may form the basis of meditation:

> It would seem that there are . . . many believers who draw particular benefit from meditation. The House of Justice suggests that for their private meditations they may wish to use the repetition of the Greatest Name, Alláh-u-Abhá, ninety-five times a day which, although not yet applied in the West, is among the Laws, Ordinances and exhortations of the Kitáb-i-Aqdas.[81]

Many of the writings of Bahá'u'lláh lend themselves to repetition, for example:

> Greater is God than every great one![82]

the refrain in the Tablet of the Holy Mariner:

Glorified be my Lord, the All-Glorious![83]

or the verse in one of the prayers for the Fast:

> Thou seest me, O my God, holding to Thy Name, the Most Holy, the Most Luminous, the Most Mighty, the Most Great, the Most Exalted, the Most Glorious, and clinging to the hem of the robe to which have clung all in this world and in the world to come.[84]

The long healing prayer of Bahá'u'lláh also provides a refrain:

> Thou the Sufficing, Thou the Healing, Thou the Abiding, O Thou Abiding One![85]

As we have seen, Bahá'u'lláh Himself suggests that one might recite the 'Remover of Difficulties' a number of times.

The obligatory prayer for the dead requires the repetition nineteen times of each of the following six verses:

> We all, verily, worship God.
> We all, verily, bow down before God.
> We all, verily, are devoted unto God.
> We all, verily, give praise unto God.
> We all, verily, yield thanks unto God.
> We all, verily, are patient in God.[86]

Chapter 4 contains a number of short passages suitable for repetition.

Others forms of recitation might include recalling the names and titles of God. Some find it helpful to bring these to mind when in difficulty or feeling down. A partial list of such names can be found at the end of this chapter.

Another form of recitation is 'counting one's blessings', recalling the attributes of God that are reflected in one.

When reciting, one may wish to adopt one of the postures prescribed in the Bahá'í writings or in other traditions.

Bringing oneself to account each day

As noted above, Bahá'u'lláh recommends that we bring ourselves to account each day. A practice of meditation could be built around this, focusing perhaps on one's deeds and on those verses in the Bahá'í writings that exhort one to acquire virtues such as patience, kindliness, trustworthiness. This can be coupled with the reading of holy scirpture in the morning and evening.

Reflection on the Word of God

As we have seen, in some forms of meditation a mantra is used that is repeated mentally rather than out loud. Thinking of the words of God while in a reflective mood – a mood created,

perhaps, by the use of soft lighting, music or
some of the techniques of relaxation – is similar.
The verses in Chapter 4 are examples of Bahá'í
writings that may be used in this way.

An example of how the word of God can be
used for meditation may be useful. In the spirit of
trying to share the words of Bahá'u'lláh with
those who are not Bahá'ís, relaxation/meditation
evenings were arranged by a local Bahá'í commu-
nity. Each evening a different form of meditation
was tried, some more successfully than others.
The most successful evenings were those that
combined some of the techniques of relaxation –
soft, non-melodic music, dimmed lights, a faint
fragrance of attar of rose, perhaps a lighted
candle – with the reading from time to time, over
the course of a hour or so, of a verse from the
Bahá'í writings by the one guiding the relaxation. Eight or ten verses were usually enough,
with the reader giving those meditating five to
fifteen minutes to ponder on each verse. The
selections in Chapter 4 were the basis of these
readings.

Music and Poetry

Some meditation systems believe that vibrations
caused by sound have an effect upon the spirit or
consciousness. 'Abdu'l-Bahá confirms this:

Music is one of the important arts. It has great

effect upon human spirit. Musical melodies are a certain something which prove to be accidental upon etheric vibrations, for voice is nothing but the expression of vibrations, which reaching the tympanum, effect the nerves of hearing. Musical melodies are, therefore, those peculiar effects produced by, or from, vibration. However, they have the keenest effect upon the spirit. In sooth, although music is a material affair, yet its tremendous effect is spiritual, and its greatest attachment is to the realm of the spirit.[87]

Bahá'u'lláh sees music as a means of uplifting the soul:

> We, verily, have made music as a ladder for your souls, a means whereby they may be lifted up unto the realm on high . . .[88]

There are many ways in which music can enhance meditation or form the basis of it. Soft, appropriate music as background to the recitation of the words of God is often heard. Some like to alternate pieces of music with readings from the scriptures. We are even encouraged by 'Abdu'l-Bahá to:

> . . . set to music the verses and the divine words so that they may be sung with soul-stirring melody in the Assemblies and gatherings, and that the hearts of the listeners may become tumultuous and rise

towards the Kingdom of Abhá in supplication and prayer.[89]

Listening to the words of God set to music, or singing them oneself, can be a satisfying form of meditation. Indeed, Shoghi Effendi

> . . . thinks it even advisable that the believers should make use, in their meetings, of hymns composed by Bahá'ís themselves, and also of such hymns, poems and chants as are based on the Holy Words.[90]

These few suggestions are only signposts to those who wish to meditate. We are left free to determine what, if any, method we will use to meditate, provided we 'guard against superstitious or foolish ideas creeping into it'.[91]

Some of the Names and Titles of God

The Able
The All-Bountiful
The All-Compelling
The All-Glorious
The All-Highest

The All-Informed
The All-Knowing
The All Merciful
The All-Perceiving
The All-Possessing

The All-Powerful
The All-Subduing
The All-Sufficing
The All-Wise
The Almighty

The Ancient
The Assister

The Beneficent
The Bestower
The Bountiful

The Changeless
The Clement
The Compassionate
The Confirmer
The Creator

The Defender
The Dispeller of every affliction
The Enlightener of all creation
The Eternal
The Eternal Truth

The Ever-Abiding
The Ever-Bestowing
The Ever-Forgiving
The Ever-Giving
The Exalted

The Faithful
The Fashioner
The Forgiver
The Generous
The Gentle

The Giver
The Glorified
The Gracious

The Great
The Guardian

The Healer
The Hearer
The Help in Peril
The Helper
The Inaccessible

The Incomparable
The Invincible
The Keeper
The Kind
The King of all men

The King of all Kings
The King of the Seen and the Unseen
The Knower
The Lightgiver
The Lord of Invincible Might

The Lord of all the worlds
The Lord of grace abounding
The Lord of Reckoning
The Lord of manifest tokens
The Loving

The Merciful of the Most Merciful
The Mighty
The Mighty Doer
The Most Benevolent

The Most Bountiful

The Most Exalted
The Most Generous
The Most Great
The Most Glorious
The Most High

The Most Holy
The Most Luminous
The Most Merciful
The Most Mighty
The Most Powerful

The Omnipotent
The Omniscient
The One
The Open of Hand
The Ordainer

The Pardoner
The Peerless
The Pitiful
The Potent
The Powerful

The Precious
The Preserver
The Protector
The Provider
The Remover of every anguish

The Seer
The Self-Subsisting
The Single
The Sovereign
The Sovereign Ruler

The Sovereign Truth
The Strong
The Subtile
The Sufficer
The Supreme Protector

The Supreme Ruler
The Sustainer
The Tender
The Unconditioned
The Unconstrained

The Unsearchable
The Unseen
The Untrammelled
The Victorious
The Wise

4
Short Verses for Meditation

The following verses have been selected from the vast ocean of the words of Bahá'u'lláh, the Báb and 'Abdu'l-Bahá as examples of how one may use the Bahá'í writings to 'turn the mirror' of our spirits 'heavenwards'. These particular words and themes have been chosen to appeal to people from all faith traditions.

Love

In thy soul of love build thou a fire
And burn all thoughts and words entire.[1]

Bahá'u'lláh

In the garden of thy heart plant naught but the rose of love . . .[2]

Bahá'u'lláh

The first sign of faith is love.[3]

'Abdu'l-Bahá

... love is light, no matter in what abode it dwelleth ... [4]

'Abdu'l-Bahá

Love is heaven's kindly light ... [5]

'Abdu'l-Bahá

Love is the one means that ensureth true felicity both in this world and the next. [6]

'Abdu'l-Bahá

Love is the light that guideth in darkness ... [7]

'Abdu'l-Bahá

Love is the most great law that ruleth this mighty and heavenly cycle ... [8]

'Abdu'l-Bahá

Love is the spirit of life unto the adorned body of mankind ... [9]

'Abdu'l-Bahá

Love is the very cause of life ... [10]

'Abdu'l-Bahá

Love is the source of all the bestowals of God. [11]

'Abdu'l-Bahá

... love is the ground of all things. [12]

'Abdu'l-Bahá

Until love takes possession of the heart, no other
divine bounty can be revealed in it.[13]

'Abdu'l-Bahá

Love must be free from boundaries![14]

'Abdu'l-Bahá

What a power is love! It is the most wonderful,
the greatest of all living powers.[15]

'Abdu'l-Bahá

Love gives life to the lifeless.[16]

'Abdu'l-Bahá

Love lights a flame in the heart that is cold.[17]

'Abdu'l-Bahá

Love brings hope to the hopeless and gladdens
the hearts of the sorrowful.[18]

'Abdu'l-Bahá

In the world of existence there is indeed no
greater power than the power of love.[19]

'Abdu'l-Bahá

. . . true love, real love, is the love for God. . .[20]

'Abdu'l-Bahá

Where there is love, nothing is too much trouble
and there is always time.[21]

'Abdu'l-Bahá

Unity

So powerful is the light of unity that it can illuminate the whole earth.[22]

Bahá'u'lláh

Ye are all the leaves of one tree and the drops of one ocean.[23]

Bahá'u'lláh

This span of earth is but one homeland and one habitation.[24]

Bahá'u'lláh

Know ye not why We created you all from the same dust? That no one should exalt himself over the other.[25]

Bahá'u'lláh

Consider the rose: whether it blossometh in the East or in the West, it is none the less a rose.[26]

Bahá'u'lláh

Recognizing Truth

. . . men of enlightened heart worship truth on whatever horizon it appears.[27]

'Abdu'l-Bahá

Light is good in whatsoever lamp it is burning! A rose is beautiful in whatsoever garden it may

bloom! A star has the same radiance if it shines
from the East or from the West.[28]

'Abdu'l-Bahá

Man must be a lover of the light no matter from
what day-spring it may appear. He must be a
lover of the rose no matter in what soil it may be
growing.[29]

'Abdu'l-Bahá

The days are many, but the sun is one. The
fountains are many, but the fountainhead is one.
The branches are many, but the tree is one.[30]

'Abdu'l-Bahá

True Life

Wert thou to attain to but a dewdrop of the
crystal waters of divine knowledge, thou wouldst
readily realize that true life is not the life of the
flesh but the life of the spirit.[31]

Bahá'u'lláh

This present life is even as a swelling wave, or a
mirage, or drifting shadows.[32]

'Abdu'l-Bahá

The pathway of life is the road which leads to
divine knowledge and attainment.[33]

'Abdu'l-Bahá

Peace

The well-being of mankind, its peace and security, are unattainable unless and until its unity is firmly established.[34]

Bahá'u'lláh

Trustworthiness is the greatest portal leading unto the tranquillity and security of the people.[35]

Bahá'u'lláh

Religion is, verily, the chief instrument for the establishment of order in the world, and of tranquillity amongst its peoples.[36]

Bahá'u'lláh

Thoughts of love are constructive of brotherhood, peace, friendship, and happiness.[37]

'Abdu'l-Bahá

Peace is light . . .[38]

'Abdu'l-Bahá

Achieving Enlightenment

Out of the essence of knowledge I gave thee being, why seekest thou enlightenment from anyone beside Me?[39]

Bahá'u'lláh

The heaven of true understanding shineth

resplendent with the light of two luminaries:
tolerance and righteousness.[40]

Bahá'u'lláh

. . . that which is the cause of everlasting life,
eternal honor, universal enlightenment, real
salvation and prosperity is, first of all, the
knowledge of God.[41]

'Abdu'l-Bahá

Spiritual progress is through the breaths of the
Holy Spirit and is the awakening of the conscious
soul of man to perceive the reality of divinity.[42]

'Abdu'l-Bahá

Spiritual progress insures the happiness and
eternal continuance of the soul.[43]

'Abdu'l-Bahá

. . . do all ye can to disengage your inner selves,
that ye may at every moment reflect new
splendours from the Sun of Truth.[44]

'Abdu'l-Bahá

Freedom

If thou art desiring divine joy, free thyself from
the bands of attachment.[45]

'Abdu'l-Bahá

If we are imprisoned in the material world, our

spirit can soar into the Heavens and we shall be free indeed![46]

'Abdu'l-Bahá

Freedom is not a matter of place, but of condition.[47]

'Abdu'l-Bahá

When one is released from the prison of self, that is, indeed, freedom. For self is the greatest prison.[48]

'Abdu'l-Bahá

Nearness to God

Meditate on what the poet hath written: 'Wonder not, if my Best-Beloved be closer to me than mine own self; wonder at this, that I, despite such nearness, should still be so far from Him.'[49]

Bahá'u'lláh

We are closer to man than his life-vein.[50]

Bahá'u'lláh

When a man turns his face to God he finds sunshine everywhere.[51]

'Abdu'l-Bahá

Our True Selves

Ye are the stars of the heaven of understanding,

the breeze that stirreth at the break of day, the
soft-flowing waters upon which must depend the
very life of all men, the letters inscribed upon His
sacred scroll.[52]

Bahá'u'lláh

Ye are the breezes of spring that are wafted over
the world.[53]

Bahá'u'lláh

Through you the countenance of the world hath
been wreathed in smiles, and the brightness of
His light shone forth.[54]

Bahá'u'lláh

In the eyes of the All-Merciful a true man
appeareth even as a firmament; its sun and moon
are his sight and hearing, and his shining and
resplendent character its stars.[55]

Bahá'u'lláh

True loss is for him whose days have been spent in
utter ignorance of his self.[56]

Bahá'u'lláh

Man's merit lieth in service and virtue and not in
the pageantry of wealth and riches.[57]

Bahá'u'lláh

The purpose of life

I bear witness, O my God, that Thou hast created me to know Thee and to worship Thee.[58]

Bahá'u'lláh

The purpose of God in creating man hath been, and will ever be, to enable him to know his Creator and to attain His Presence.[59]

Bahá'u'lláh

The purpose of the creation of man is the attainment of the supreme virtues of humanity through descent of the heavenly bestowals.[60]

'Abdu'l-Bahá

The purpose of man's creation is, therefore, unity and harmony . . . [61]

'Abdu'l-Bahá

The Soul

Know, verily, that the soul is a sign of God, a heavenly gem . . . [62]

Bahá'u'lláh

Verily I say, the human soul is exalted above all egress and regress. It is still, and yet it soareth; it moveth, and yet it is still.[63]

Bahá'u'lláh

Developing Spiritual Qualities

The light of a good character surpasseth the light of the sun and the radiance thereof.[64]

Bahá'u'lláh

A kindly tongue is the lodestone of the hearts of men.[65]

Bahá'u'lláh

Be thou patient and quiet thyself. The things thou desirest can last but an hour.[66]

Bahá'u'lláh

If thou art seeking everlasting glory, choose humility in the path of the True One.[67]

'Abdu'l-Bahá

Sacrifice

If thou art aspiring to eternal life, sacrifice thy soul in the way of God.[68]

'Abdu'l-Bahá

. . . nearness to God necessitates sacrifice of self, severance and the giving up of all to Him.[69]

'Abdu'l-Bahá

One of the requirements of faithfulness is that thou mayest sacrifice thyself . . .[70]

'Abdu'l-Bahá

To make a sacrifice is to receive a gift . . .[71]

'Abdu'l-Bahá

This is the true sacrifice: the offering of oneself, even as did Christ, as a ransom for the life of the world.[72]

'Abdu'l-Bahá

. . . this plane of sacrifice is the realm of dying to the self, that the radiance of the living God may then shine forth.[73]

'Abdu'l-Bahá

The mystery of sacrifice is that man should sacrifice all his conditions for the divine station of God.[74]

'Abdu'l-Bahá

Self-empowerment

Let each morn be better than its eve and each morrow richer than its yesterday.[75]

Bahá'u'lláh

Be unto the world as rain and clouds of mercy, as suns of truth; be a celestial army, and you shall indeed conquer the city of hearts.[76]

'Abdu'l-Bahá

Endeavour with thy soul, so that the fountain of knowledge may flow within thy heart and the

bounties of mysteries may pour upon thee from
the Kingdom of Lights.[77]

'Abdu'l-Bahá

Suffering

Verily God hath made adversity as a morning dew
upon His green pasture, and a wick for His lamp
which lighteth earth and heaven.[78]

Bahá'u'lláh

Those who suffer most, attain to the greatest
perfection.[79]

'Abdu'l-Bahá

The plant most pruned by the gardeners is that
one which, when the summer comes, will have the
most beautiful blossoms and the most abundant
fruit.[80]

'Abdu'l-Bahá

Grief and sorrow do not come to us by chance,
they are sent to us by the Divine Mercy for our
own perfecting.[81]

'Abdu'l-Bahá

Hope

Nothing is impossible to the Divine Benevolence
of God . . .[82]

'Abdu'l-Bahá

. . . with eyes of faith look into the future, for in truth the Spirit of God is working in your midst.[83]

'Abdu'l-Bahá

A seed in the beginning is very small, but in the end a great tree. One should not consider the seed, but the tree and its abundance of blossoms, leaves and fruits.[84]

'Abdu'l-Bahá

Happiness

True happiness depends on spiritual good and having the heart ever open to receive the Divine Bounty.[85]

'Abdu'l-Bahá

Man is, in reality, a spiritual being, and only when he lives in the spirit is he truly happy.[86]

'Abdu'l-Bahá

When we find truth, constancy, fidelity, and love, we are happy . . .[87]

'Abdu'l-Bahá

If we are not happy and joyous at this season, for what other season shall we wait and for what other time shall we look?[88]

'Abdu'l-Bahá

5

Longer Meditations

Many of Bahá'u'lláh's writings are meditations in themselves. A small number appear here as an example.

On God

Mine eyes are cheered, O my God, when I contemplate the tribulations that descend upon me from the heaven of Thy decree, and which have encompassed me on every side according to what Thy pen hath irrevocably established. I swear by Thy Self! Whatsoever is of Thee is well pleasing unto me, though it involve the bitterness of mine own death.

He Who was Thy Spirit (Jesus), O my God, withdrew all alone in the darkness of the night preceding His last day on earth, and falling on His face to the ground besought Thee saying: 'If it be Thy will, O my Lord, my Well-Beloved, let this cup, through Thy grace and bounty, pass from me.'

By Thy beauty, O Thou Who art the Lord of all names and the Creator of the heavens! I can smell the fragrance of the words which, in His love for Thee, His lips have uttered, and can feel the glow of the fire that had inflamed His soul in its longing to behold Thy face and in its yearning after the Day-Spring of the light of Thy oneness, and the Dawning-Place of Thy transcendent unity.

As to me – and to this Thou art Thyself my witness – I call upon Thee saying: 'I have no will of mine own, O my Lord, and my Master and my Ruler, before the indications of Thy will, and can have no purpose in the face of the revelation of Thy purpose. I swear by Thy glory! I wish only what Thou wishest, and cherish only what Thou cherishest. What I have chosen for myself is what Thou hast Thyself chosen for me, O Thou the Possessor of my soul!' Nay, I find myself to be altogether nothing when face to face with the manifold revelations of Thy names, how much less when confronted with the effulgent splendours of the light of Thine own Self. O miserable me! Were I to attempt merely to describe Thee, such an attempt would itself be an evidence of my impiety, and would attest my heedlessness in the face of the clear and resplendent tokens of Thy oneness. Who else except Thee can claim to be worthy of any notice

in the face of Thine own revelation, and who is he
that can be deemed sufficiently qualified to
adequately praise Thee, or to pride himself on
having befittingly described Thy glory? Nay –
and to this Thou dost Thyself bear witness – it
hath incontrovertibly been made evident that
Thou art the one God, the Incomparable, Whose
help is implored by all men. From everlasting
Thou wert alone, with none to describe Thee,
and wilt abide forever the same with no one else
to equal or rival Thee. Were the existence of any
co-equal with Thee to be recognized, how could
it then be maintained that Thou art the
Incomparable, or that Thy Godhead is
immeasurably exalted above all peers or likeness?
The contemplation of the highest minds that
have recognized Thy unity failed to attain unto
the comprehension of the One Thou hast created
through the word of Thy commandment, how
much more must it be powerless to soar into the
atmosphere of the knowledge of Thine own
Being. Every praise which any tongue or pen can
recount, every imagination which any heart can
devise, is debarred from the station which Thy
most exalted Pen hath ordained, how much more
must it fall short of the heights which Thou hast
Thyself immensely exalted above the conception
and the description of any creature. For the
attempt of the evanescent to conceive the signs of
the Uncreated is as the stirring of the drop before
the tumult of Thy billowing oceans. Nay, forbid

it, O my God, that I should thus venture to describe Thee, for every similitude and comparison must pertain to what is essentially created by Thee. How can then such similitude and comparison ever befit Thee, or reach up unto Thy Self?

By Thy glory, O my God! Though I recognize and firmly believe that no description which any except Thyself can give of Thee can beseem Thy grandeur, and that no glory ascribed to Thee by any save Thyself can ever ascend into the atmosphere of Thy presence, yet were I to hold my peace, and cease to glorify Thee and to recount Thy wondrous glory, my heart would be consumed, and my soul would melt away.

My remembrance of Thee, O my God, quencheth my thirst, and quieteth my heart. My soul delighteth in its communion with Thee, as the sucking child delighteth itself in the breasts of Thy mercy; and my heart panteth after Thee even as one sore athirst panteth after the living waters of Thy bounty, O Thou Who art the God of mercy, in Whose hand is the lordship of all things!

I give thanks to Thee, O my God, that Thou hast suffered me to remember Thee. What else but remembrance of Thee can give delight to my soul or gladness to my heart? Communion with Thee enableth me to dispense with the remembrance of all Thy creatures, and my love for Thee empowereth me to endure the harm which my oppressors inflict upon me.

Send, therefore, unto my loved ones, O my God, what will cheer their hearts, and illumine their faces, and delight their souls. Thou knowest, O my Lord, that their joy is to behold the exaltation of Thy Cause and the glorification of Thy word. Do Thou unveil, therefore, O my God, what will gladden their eyes, and ordain for them the good of this world and of the world which is to come.

Thou art, verily, the God of power, of strength and of bounty.[1]

In Glorification of God

Praise be to Thee, to Whom the tongues of all created things have, from eternity, called, and yet failed to attain the heaven of Thine eternal holiness and grandeur. The eyes of all beings have been opened to behold the beauty of Thy radiant countenance, yet none hath succeeded in gazing on the brightness of the light of Thy face. The hands of them that are nigh unto Thee have, ever since the foundation of Thy glorious sovereignty and the establishment of Thy holy dominion, been raised suppliantly towards Thee, yet no one hath been able to touch the hem of the robe that clotheth Thy Divine and sovereign Essence. And yet none can deny that Thou hast ever been, through the wonders of Thy generosity and bounty, supreme over all things, art powerful to do all things, and art nearer unto all things than they are unto themselves.

Far be it, then, from Thy glory that anyone should gaze on Thy wondrous beauty with any eye save Thine own eye, or hear the melodies proclaiming Thine almighty sovereignty with any ear except Thine own ear. Too high art Thou exalted for the eye of any creature to behold Thy beauty, or for the understanding of any heart to scale the heights of Thine immeasurable knowledge. For should the birds of the hearts of them that are nigh unto Thee be ever enabled to soar as long as Thine own overpowering sovereignty can endure, or to ascend as long as the empire of Thy Divine holiness can last, they shall, in no wise, be able to transcend the limitations which a contingent world hath imposed upon them, nor pass beyond its confines. How, then, can he whose very creation is restricted by such limitations, attain unto Him Who is the Lord of the Kingdom of all created things, or ascend into the heaven of Him Who ruleth the realms of loftiness and grandeur?

Glorified, immeasurably glorified art Thou, my Best-Beloved! Inasmuch as Thou hast ordained that the utmost limit to which they who lift their hearts to Thee can rise is the confession of their powerlessness to enter the realms of Thy holy and transcendent unity, and that the highest station which they who aspire to know Thee can reach is the acknowledgment of their impotence to attain the retreats of Thy sublime knowledge I, therefore, beseech Thee, by this very powerlessness which is beloved of Thee, and which Thou hast decreed as the goal of them that have reached and attained Thy court, and by the splendours of Thy countenance that have encompassed all things, and by the energies of Thy Will whereby the entire creation hath been generated, not to deprive them that have set their hopes in Thee of the wonders of Thy mercy, nor to withhold from such as have sought Thee the treasures of Thy grace. Ignite, then, within their hearts the torch of Thy love, that its flame may consume all else except their wondrous remembrance of Thee, and that no trace may be left in those hearts except the gem-like evidences of Thy most holy sovereignty, so that from the land wherein they dwell no voice may be heard except the voice that extolleth Thy mercifulness and might, that on the earth on which they walk no light may shine except the light of Thy beauty, and that within every soul naught may be discovered except the revelation of Thy countenance and the tokens of Thy glory, that haply Thy servants may show forth only that which shall please Thee and shall conform wholly unto Thy most potent will.

Glory be to Thee, O my God! The power of Thy might beareth me witness! I can have no doubt that should the holy breaths of Thy loving-kindness and the breeze of Thy bountiful favour cease, for less than the twinkling of an eye, to breathe over all created things, the entire

creation would perish, and all that are in heaven
and on earth would be reduced to utter
nothingness. Magnified, therefore, be the
marvellous evidences of Thy transcendent power!
Magnified be the potency of Thine exalted might!
Magnified be the majesty of Thine
all-encompassing greatness, and the energizing
influence of Thy will! Such is Thy greatness that
wert Thou to concentrate the eyes of all men in
the eye of one of Thy servants, and to compress
all their hearts within his heart, and wert Thou to
enable him to behold within himself all the things
Thou hast created through Thy power and
fashioned through Thy might, and were he to
ponder, throughout eternity, over the realms of
Thy creation and the range of Thy handiwork, he
would unfailingly discover that there is no created
thing but is overshadowed by Thine
all-conquering power, and is vitalized through
Thine all-embracing sovereignty.

Behold me, then, O my God, fallen prostrate
upon the dust before Thee, confessing my
powerlessness and Thine omnipotence, my
poverty and Thy wealth, mine evanescence and
Thine eternity, mine utter abasement and Thine
infinite glory. I recognize that there is none other
God but Thee, that Thou hast no peer nor
partner, none to equal or rival Thee. In Thine
unapproachable loftiness Thou hast, from
eternity, been exalted above the praise of any one
but Thee, and shalt continue for ever, in Thy

transcendent singleness and glory, to be sanctified
from the glorification of any one except Thine
own Self.

I swear by Thy might, O my Beloved! To make
mention of any created thing beseemeth not Thy
most exalted Self, and to bestow any praise upon
anyone of Thy creatures would be wholly
unworthy of Thy great glory. Nay, such a mention
would be but blasphemy uttered within the court
of Thy holiness, and such praise would amount
to no less than a transgression in the face of the
evidences of Thy Divine sovereignty. For the mere
mention of any one of Thy creatures would in
itself imply an assertion of their existence before
the court of Thy singleness and unity. Such an
assertion would be naught but open blasphemy,
an act of impiety, the essence of profanity and a
wanton crime.

Wherefore, I bear witness with my soul, my
spirit, my entire being, that should They Who are
the Day-Springs of Thy most holy unity and the
Manifestations of Thy transcendent oneness be
able to soar so long as Thine own sovereignty
endureth and Thine all-compelling authority can
last, they will fail in the end to attain unto even
the precincts of the court wherein Thou didst
reveal the effulgence of but one of Thy most
mighty Names. Glorified, glorified be, therefore,
Thy wondrous majesty. Glorified, glorified be
Thine unattainable loftiness. Glorified, glorified
be the preeminence of Thy kingship and the

sublimity of Thine authority and power.

The highest faculties which the learned have possessed, and whatsoever truths they, in their search after the gems of Thy knowledge, have discovered; the brightest realities with which the wise have been endowed, and whatever secrets they, in their attempts to fathom the mysteries of Thy wisdom, have unravelled, have all been created through the generative power of the Spirit that was breathed into the Pen which Thy hands have fashioned. How, then, can the thing which Thy Pen hath created be capable of comprehending those treasures of Thy Faith with which, as decreed by Thee, that Pen hath been invested? How can it ever know of the Fingers that grasp Thy Pen, and of Thy merciful favours with which it hath been endowed? How can it, already unable to reach this station, be made aware of the existence of Thy Hand that controlleth the Fingers of Thy might? How can it attain unto the comprehension of the nature of Thy Will that animateth the movement of Thy Hand?

Glorified, glorified be Thou, O my God! How can I ever hope to ascend into the heaven of Thy most holy will, or gain admittance into the tabernacle of Thy Divine knowledge, knowing as I do that the minds of the wise and learned are impotent to fathom the secrets of Thy handiwork – a handiwork which is itself but a creation of Thy will?

Praise be to Thee, O Lord, my God, my Master, my Possessor, my King. Now that I have confessed unto Thee my powerlessness and the powerlessness of all created things, and have acknowledged my poverty and the poverty of the entire creation, I call unto Thee with my tongue and the tongues of all that are in heaven and on earth, and beseech Thee with my heart and the hearts of all that have entered beneath the shadow of Thy names and Thine attributes, not to shut us from the doors of Thy loving-kindness and grace, nor to suffer the breeze of Thy bountiful care and favour to cease from being wafted over our souls, nor to permit that our hearts be occupied with anyone except Thee, or our minds to be busied with any remembrance save remembrance of Thy Self.

By the glory of Thy might, O my God! Wert Thou to set me king over Thy realms, and to establish me upon the throne of Thy sovereignty, and to deliver, through Thy power, the reins of the entire creation into my hands, and wert Thou to cause me, though it be for less than a moment, to be occupied with these things and be oblivious of the wondrous memories associated with Thy most mighty, most perfect, and most exalted Name, my soul would still remain unsatisfied, and the pangs of my heart unstilled. Nay, I would, in that very state, recognize myself as the poorest of the poor, and the most wretched of the wretched.

Magnified be Thy name, O my God! Now that Thou hast caused me to apprehend this truth, I beseech Thee by Thy Name which no scroll can bear, which no heart can imagine and no tongue can utter – a Name which will remain concealed so long as Thine own Essence is hidden, and will be glorified so long as Thine own Being is extolled – to unfurl, ere the present year draw to a close, the ensigns of Thine undisputed ascendancy and triumph, that the whole creation may be enriched by Thy wealth, and may be exalted through the ennobling influence of Thy transcendent sovereignty, and that all may arise and promote Thy Cause.

Thou art, verily, the Almighty, the All-Highest, the All-Glorious, the All-Subduing, the All-Possessing.[2]

On the Suffering of Bahá'u'lláh

Glorified art Thou, O Lord my God! Thou seest me dwelling in this prison-house that lieth behind the seas and the mountains, and knowest full well what I have endured for love of Thee and for the sake of Thy Cause. Thou art He, O my God, Who hath raised me up at Thy behest, and bidden me to occupy Thy seat, and to summon all men to the court of Thy mercy. It is Thou Who hast commanded me to tell out the things Thou didst destine for them in the Tablet of Thy decree and didst inscribe with the pen of Thy Revelation,

and Who hast enjoined on me the duty of
kindling the fire of Thy love in the hearts of Thy
servants, and of drawing all the peoples of the
earth nearer to the habitation of Thy throne.

And when, as bidden by Thee, I arose and called
out, by Thy leave, all Thy creatures, the wayward
among Thy servants opposed me. Some turned
away from me, others disowned my claim, a few
hesitated, while others were sore perplexed,
notwithstanding that Thy testimony was set forth
before the followers of all religions, and Thy proof
demonstrated unto all the peoples of the earth,
and the signs of Thy might so powerfully
manifested as to encompass the entire creation.

I was, moreover, opposed by mine own kindred,
although, as Thou knowest, they were dear to me
and I had desired for them that which I had
desired for mine own self. These are the ones
who, when learning that I had been cast into
prison, perpetrated against me what no man else
on earth had perpetrated.

I entreat Thee, therefore, O my God, by Thy
name by which Thou hast separated between
truth and denial, to purify their hearts of all evil
suggestions, and to enable them to draw nigh
unto Him Who is the Day-Spring of Thy names
and Thine attributes.

Thou knowest, O my God, that I have severed
every tie that bindeth me to any of Thy creatures
except that most exalted tie that uniteth me with
whosoever cleaveth unto Thee, in this the day of

the revelation of Thy most august Self, that hath appeared in Thy name, the All-Glorious. Thou knowest that I have dissolved every bond that knitteth me to any one of my kindred except such as have enjoyed near access to Thy most effulgent face.

I have no will but Thy will, O my Lord, and cherish no desire except Thy desire. From my pen floweth only the summons which Thine own exalted pen hath voiced, and my tongue uttereth naught save what the Most Great Spirit hath itself proclaimed in the kingdom of Thine eternity. I am stirred by nothing else except the winds of Thy will, and breathe no word except the words which, by Thy leave and Thine inspiration, I am led to pronounce.

Praise be to Thee, O Thou Who art the Well-Beloved of all that have known Thee, and the Desire of the hearts of such as are devoted to Thee, inasmuch as Thou hast made me a target for the ills that I suffer in my love for Thee, and the object of the assaults launched against me in Thy path. Thy glory beareth me witness! I can, on no account, feel impatient of the adversities that I have borne in my love for Thee. From the very day Thou didst reveal Thyself unto me, I have accepted for myself every manner of tribulation. Every moment of my life my head crieth out to Thee and saith: 'Would, O my Lord, that I could be raised on the spear-point in Thy path!' while my blood entreateth Thee saying: 'Dye the earth with me, O my God, for the sake of Thy love and Thy pleasure!' Thou knowest that I have, at no time, sought to guard my body against any affliction, nay rather I have continually anticipated the things Thou didst ordain for me in the Tablet of Thy decree.

Behold, then, O my God, my loneliness among Thy servants and my remoteness from Thy friends and Thy chosen ones. I beseech Thee, by the showers of the clouds of Thy mercy, whereby Thou hast caused the blossoms of Thy praise and utterance and the flowers of Thy wisdom and testimony to spring forth in the hearts of all them that have recognized Thy oneness, to supply Thy servants and my kindred with the fruits of the tree of Thy unity, in these days when Thou hast been established upon the throne of Thy mercy. Hinder them not, O my Lord, from attaining unto the things Thou dost possess, and write down for them that which will aid them to scale the heights of Thy grace and favour. Give them, moreover, to drink of the living waters of Thy knowledge, and ordain for them the good of this world and of the world to come.

Thou art, verily, the Lord of Bahá, and the Beloved of his heart, and the Object of his desire, and the Inspirer of his tongue, and the Source of his soul. No God is there but Thee, the Inaccessible, the Most High. Thou art, verily, the Almighty, the Most Exalted, the Ever-Forgiving, the Most Merciful.[3]

6
'Ponder This in Thy Heart'

Bahá'u'lláh identifies a number of themes worthy of our reflection. Here are a few examples from His writings.

The Majesty of God

I swear by Thy glory, O Beloved of my soul! I am bewildered when I contemplate the tokens of Thy handiwork, and the evidences of Thy might, and find myself completely unable to unravel the mystery of the least of Thy signs, how much more to apprehend Thine own Self.[1]

In the Name of God, the Clement, the Merciful.
Praise be to God Who hath made being to come forth from nothingness; graven upon the tablet of man the secrets of preexistence; taught him from the mysteries of divine utterance that which he knew not; made him a Luminous Book unto those

who believed and surrendered themselves; caused
him to witness the creation of all things . . . in this
black and ruinous age, and to speak forth from
the apex of eternity with a wondrous voice in the
Excellent Temple: to the end that every man may
testify, in himself, by himself, in the station of the
Manifestation of his Lord, that verily there is no
God save Him, and that every man may thereby
win his way to the summit of realities, until none
shall contemplate anything whatsoever but that
he shall see God therein.[2]

By Thy life, O Thou the Possessor of all names!
The minds of the profoundest thinkers are sore
perplexed as they contemplate the ocean of Thy
knowledge, and the heaven of Thy wisdom, and
the Luminary of Thy grace. How can he who is
but a creation of Thy will claim to know what is
with Thee, or to conceive Thy nature?[3]

Purify me of all that is not of Thee, and
strengthen me to love Thee and to fulfill Thy
pleasure, that I may delight myself in the
contemplation of Thy beauty, and be rid of all
attachment to any of Thy creatures, and may, at
every moment, proclaim: 'Magnified be God, the
Lord of the worlds!'[4]

They whose sight is keen, whose ears are
retentive, whose hearts are enlightened, and
whose breasts are dilated, recognize both truth

and falsehood, and distinguish the one from the other. Recite thou this prayer that hath flowed from the tongue of this Wronged One, and ponder thereon with a heart rid of all attachment, and with ears that are pure and sanctified, be attentive to its meaning, that haply thou mayest inhale the breath of detachment and have pity upon thyself and upon others:

'My God, the Object of my adoration, the Goal of my desire, the All-Bountiful, the Most Compassionate! All life is of Thee, and all power lieth within the grasp of Thine omnipotence. Whosoever Thou exaltest is raised above the angels, and attaineth the station: "Verily, We uplifted him to a place on high!" and whosoever Thou dost abase is made lower than dust, nay, less than nothing. O Divine Providence! Though wicked, sinful and intemperate, we still seek from Thee a "seat of truth", and long to behold the countenance of the Omnipotent King.

It is Thine to command, and all sovereignty belongeth to Thee, and the realm of might boweth before Thy behest. Everything Thou doest is pure justice, nay, the very essence of grace. One gleam from the splendors of Thy Name, the All-Merciful, sufficeth to banish and blot out every trace of sinfulness from the world, and a single breath from the breezes of the Day of Thy Revelation is enough to adorn all mankind with a fresh attire. Vouchsafe Thy strength, O Almighty One, unto Thy weak creatures, and quicken them who are as dead, that haply they may find Thee, and may be led unto the ocean of Thy guidance, and may remain steadfast in Thy Cause.

Should the fragrance of Thy praise be shed abroad by any of the divers tongues of the world, out of the East or out of the West, it would, verily, be prized and greatly cherished. If such tongues, however, be deprived of that fragrance, they assuredly would be unworthy of any mention, in word or yet in thought. We beg of Thee, O Providence, to show Thy way unto all men, and to guide them aright. Thou art, verily, the Almighty, the Most Powerful, the All-Knowing, the All-Seeing.'⁵

The Power of God

Behold, how many are the mysteries that lie as yet unravelled within the tabernacle of the knowledge of God, and how numerous the gems of His wisdom that are still concealed in His inviolable treasuries! Shouldest thou ponder this in thine heart, thou wouldst realize that His handiwork knoweth neither beginning nor end. The domain of His decree is too vast for the tongue of mortals to describe, or for the bird of the human mind to traverse; and the dispensations of His providence are too mysterious for the mind of man to comprehend. His creation no end hath overtaken, and it hath ever existed from the 'Beginning that hath no beginning'; and the Manifestations of His Beauty no beginning hath beheld, and they will continue to the 'End that knoweth no end'. Ponder this utterance in thine heart, and reflect how it is applicable unto all these holy Souls.[6]

The Power of the Word of God

Do thou ponder on the penetrative influence of the Word of God.[7]

Ponder, now, O Shaykh, the influence of the word of God, that haply thou mayest turn from the left hand of idle fancy unto the right hand of certitude.[8]

The breeze of the bounty of the King of creation hath caused even the physical earth to be changed, were ye to ponder in your hearts the mysteries of divine Revelation.[9]

Detachment from All Save God

The heart must needs therefore be cleansed from the idle sayings of men, and sanctified from every earthly affection, so that it may discover the hidden meaning of divine inspiration, and become the treasury of the mysteries of divine knowledge. Thus hath it been said: 'He that treadeth the snow-white Path, and followeth in the footsteps of the Crimson Pillar, shall never attain unto his abode unless his hands are empty of those worldly things cherished by men.' This is the prime requisite of whosoever treadeth this path. Ponder thereon, that, with eyes unveiled, thou mayest perceive the truth of these words.[10]

O My Friend in Word! Ponder awhile. Hast thou ever heard that friend and foe should abide in one heart? Cast out then the stranger, that the Friend may enter His home.[11]

Sacrifice for the Sake of God

O Son of Man! Ponder and reflect. Is it thy wish to die upon thy bed, or to shed thy life-blood on the dust, a martyr in My path, and so become the manifestation of My command and the revealer of My light in the highest paradise? Judge thou aright, O servant![12]

Progressive Revelation

Contemplate with thine inward eye the chain of successive Revelations that hath linked the Manifestation of Adam with that of the Báb. I testify before God that each one of these Manifestations hath been sent down through the operation of the Divine Will and Purpose, that each hath been the bearer of a specific Message, that each hath been entrusted with a divinely-revealed Book and been commissioned to unravel the mysteries of a mighty Tablet. The measure of the Revelation with which every one of them hath been identified had been definitely fore-ordained. This, verily, is a token of Our favour unto them, if ye be of those that comprehend this truth . . . And when this process of progressive Revelation culminated in the stage at which His peerless, His most sacred, and exalted Countenance was to be unveiled to men's eyes, He chose to hide His own Self behind a thousand veils, lest profane and mortal eyes discover His glory. This He did at a time when the signs and tokens of a divinely-appointed Revelation were being showered upon Him – signs and tokens which none can reckon except the Lord, your God, the Lord of all worlds. And when the set time of concealment was fulfilled, We sent forth, whilst still wrapt within a myriad veils, an infinitesimal glimmer of the effulgent Glory enveloping the Face of the Youth, and lo, the entire company of the dwellers of the Realms above were seized with violent commotion and the favoured of God fell down in adoration before Him. He hath, verily, manifested a glory such as none in the whole creation hath witnessed, inasmuch as He hath arisen to proclaim in person His Cause unto all who are in the heavens and all who are on the earth.[13]

Now is the moment in which to cleanse thyself
with the waters of detachment that have flowed
out from the Supreme Pen, and to ponder, wholly
for the sake of God, those things which, time and
again, have been sent down or manifested, and
then to strive, as much as lieth in thee, to quench,
through the power of wisdom and the force of
thy utterance, the fire of enmity and hatred which
smouldereth in the hearts of the peoples of the
world. The Divine Messengers have been sent
down, and their Books were revealed, for the
purpose of promoting the knowledge of God,
and of furthering unity and fellowship amongst
men. But now behold, how they have made the
Law of God a cause and pretext for perversity
and hatred. How pitiful, how regrettable, that
most men are cleaving fast to, and have busied
themselves with, the things they possess, and are
unaware of, and shut out as by a veil from, the
things God possesseth![14]

Recognition of the Manifestation of God

. . . every man hath been, and will continue to be,
able of himself to appreciate the Beauty of God,
the Glorified. Had he not been endowed with
such a capacity, how could he be called to account
for his failure? If, in the Day when all the peoples
of the earth will be gathered together, any man
should, whilst standing in the presence of God,

be asked: 'Wherefore hast thou disbelieved in My
Beauty and turned away from My Self', and if
such a man should reply and say: 'Inasmuch as all
men have erred, and none hath been found
willing to turn his face to the Truth, I, too,
following their example, have grievously failed to
recognize the Beauty of the Eternal', such a plea
will, assuredly, be rejected. For the faith of no
man can be conditioned by any one except
himself. This is one of the verities that lie
enshrined in My Revelation – a verity which I
have revealed in all the heavenly Books, which I
have caused the Tongue of Grandeur to utter, and
the Pen of Power to inscribe. Ponder a while
thereon, that with both your inner and outer eye,
ye may perceive the subtleties of Divine wisdom
and discover the gems of heavenly knowledge
which, in clear and weighty language, I have
revealed in this exalted and incorruptible Tablet,
and that ye may not stray far from the
All-Highest Throne, from the Tree beyond which
there is no passing, from the Habitation of
everlasting might and glory.[15]

His Revelation

O heedless ones! Though the wonders of My
mercy have encompassed all created things, both
visible and invisible, and though the revelations
of My grace and bounty have permeated every
atom of the universe, yet the rod with which I can

chastise the wicked is grievous, and the fierceness of Mine anger against them terrible. With ears that are sanctified from vain-glory and worldly desires hearken unto the counsels which I, in My merciful kindness, have revealed unto you, and with your inner and outer eyes contemplate the evidences of My marvelous Revelation . . . [16]

With fixed and steady gaze, born of the unerring eye of God, scan for a while the horizon of divine knowledge, and contemplate those words of perfection which the Eternal hath revealed, that haply the mysteries of divine wisdom, hidden ere now beneath the veil of glory and treasured within the tabernacle of His grace, may be made manifest unto you.[17]

Would that ye might ponder the Cause of God in your hearts![18]

The Suffering of Bahá'u'lláh

By the righteousness of God! Every morning I arose from My bed, I discovered the hosts of countless afflictions massed behind My door; and every night when I lay down, lo! My heart was torn with agony at what it had suffered from the fiendish cruelty of its foes. With every piece of bread the Ancient Beauty breaketh is coupled the assault of a fresh affliction, and with every drop

He drinketh is mixed the bitterness of the most woeful of trials. He is preceded in every step He taketh by an army of unforeseen calamities, while in His rear follow legions of agonizing sorrows. Such is My plight, wert thou to ponder it in thine heart. Let not, however, thy soul grieve over that which God hath rained down upon Us. Merge thy will in His pleasure, for We have, at no time, desired anything whatsoever except His Will, and have welcomed each one of His irrevocable decrees. Let thine heart be patient, and be thou not dismayed. Follow not in the way of them that are sorely agitated.[19]

The Nature of the Soul

Verily I say, the human soul is, in its essence, one of the signs of God, a mystery among His mysteries. It is one of the mighty signs of the Almighty, the harbinger that proclaimeth the reality of all the worlds of God. Within it lieth concealed that which the world is now utterly incapable of apprehending. Ponder in thine heart the revelation of the Soul of God that pervadeth all His Laws, and contrast it with that base and appetitive nature that hath rebelled against Him, that forbiddeth men to turn unto the Lord of Names, and impelleth them to walk after their lusts and wickedness. Such a soul hath, in truth, wandered far in the path of error . . .[20]

Creation

Witness the wondrous evidences of God's handiwork, and reflect upon its range and character. He Who is the Seal of the Prophets hath said: 'Increase my wonder and amazement at Thee, O God!'[21]

The Worlds of Creation

As to thy question concerning the worlds of God. Know thou of a truth that the worlds of God are countless in their number, and infinite in their range. None can reckon or comprehend them except God, the All-Knowing, the All-Wise. Consider thy state when asleep. Verily, I say, this phenomenon is the most mysterious of the signs of God amongst men, were they to ponder it in their hearts. Behold how the thing which thou hast seen in thy dream is, after a considerable lapse of time, fully realized. Had the world in which thou didst find thyself in thy dream been identical with the world in which thou livest, it would have been necessary for the event occurring in that dream to have transpired in this world at the very moment of its occurrence. Were it so, you yourself would have borne witness unto it. This being not the case, however, it must necessarily follow that the world in which thou livest is different and apart from that which thou hast experienced in thy dream. This latter world hath neither beginning nor end. It would be true if thou

wert to contend that this same world is, as decreed
by the All-Glorious and Almighty God, within thy
proper self and is wrapped up within thee. It
would equally be true to maintain that thy spirit,
having transcended the limitations of sleep and
having stripped itself of all earthly attachment,
hath, by the act of God, been made to traverse a
realm which lieth hidden in the innermost reality
of this world. Verily I say, the creation of God
embraceth worlds besides this world, and
creatures apart from these creatures. In each of
these worlds He hath ordained things which none
can search except Himself, the All-Searching, the
All-Wise. Do thou meditate on that which We
have revealed unto thee, that thou mayest discover
the purpose of God, thy Lord, and the Lord of all
worlds. In these words the mysteries of Divine
Wisdom have been treasured.[22]

The world beyond is as different from this world
as this world is different from that of the child
while still in the womb of its mother. When the
soul attaineth the Presence of God, it will assume
the form that best befitteth its immortality and is
worthy of its celestial habitation. Such an
existence is a contingent and not an absolute
existence, inasmuch as the former is preceded by
a cause, whilst the latter is independent thereof.
Absolute existence is strictly confined to God,
exalted be His glory. Well is it with them that
apprehend this truth. Wert thou to ponder in

thine heart the behaviour of the Prophets of God thou wouldst assuredly and readily testify that there must needs be other worlds besides this world. The majority of the truly wise and learned have, throughout the ages, as it hath been recorded by the Pen of Glory in the Tablet of Wisdom, borne witness to the truth of that which the holy Writ of God hath revealed. Even the materialists have testified in their writings to the wisdom of these divinely-appointed Messengers, and have regarded the references made by the Prophets to Paradise, to hell fire, to future reward and punishment, to have been actuated by a desire to educate and uplift the souls of men. Consider, therefore, how the generality of mankind, whatever their beliefs or theories, have recognized the excellence, and admitted the superiority, of these Prophets of God. These Gems of Detachment are acclaimed by some as the embodiments of wisdom, while others believe them to be the mouthpiece of God Himself. How could such Souls have consented to surrender themselves unto their enemies if they believed all the worlds of God to have been reduced to this earthly life? Would they have willingly suffered such afflictions and torments as no man hath ever experienced or witnessed?[23]

The World of Dreams

Behold how the dream thou hast dreamed is, after

the lapse of many years, re-enacted before thine eyes. Consider how strange is the mystery of the world that appeareth to thee in thy dream. Ponder in thine heart upon the unsearchable wisdom of God, and meditate on its manifold revelations . . .[24]

The Oneness of Humanity

O Children of Men! Know ye not why We created you all from the same dust? That no one should exalt himself over the other. Ponder at all times in your hearts how ye were created.[25]

Justice

O Son of Spirit! The best beloved of all things in My sight is Justice; turn not away therefrom if thou desirest Me, and neglect it not that I may confide in thee. By its aid thou shalt see with thine own eyes and not through the eyes of others, and shalt know of thine own knowledge and not through the knowledge of thy neighbour. Ponder this in thy heart; how it behooveth thee to be. Verily justice is My gift to thee and the sign of My loving-kindness. Set it then before thine eyes.[26]

Service in the Path of God

Beseech ye the one true God to grant that ye may taste the savour of such deeds as are performed in

His path, and partake of the sweetness of such humility and submissiveness as are shown for His sake. Forget your own selves, and turn your eyes towards your neighbour. Bend your energies to whatever may foster the education of men. Nothing is, or can ever be, hidden from God. If ye follow in His way, His incalculable and imperishable blessings will be showered upon you. This is the luminous Tablet, whose verses have streamed from the moving Pen of Him Who is the Lord of all worlds. Ponder it in your hearts, and be ye of them that observe its precepts.[27]

7
'Great Questions'

In His talk to the Society of Friends in 1913 'Abdu'l-Bahá suggested a number of 'great questions' that meditation might answer:

> Some of the great questions unfolding from the rays of the Sun of Reality upon the mind of man are: the problem of the reality of the spirit of man; of the birth of the spirit; of its birth from this world into the world of God; the question of the inner life of the spirit and of its fate after its ascension from the body.[1]

The following selections from the Bahá'í writings show how they might form the basis of one's meditation on these questions.

The Reality of the Spirit of Man

Thou hast asked Me concerning the nature of the soul. Know, verily, that the soul is a sign of God, a

heavenly gem whose reality the most learned of
men hath failed to grasp, and whose mystery no
mind, however acute, can ever hope to unravel. It
is the first among all created things to declare the
excellence of its Creator, the first to recognize His
glory, to cleave to His truth, and to bow down in
adoration before Him. If it be faithful to God, it
will reflect His light, and will, eventually, return
unto Him. If it fail, however, in its allegiance to
its Creator, it will become a victim to self and
passion, and will, in the end, sink in their depths.[2]

Bahá'u'lláh

Verily I say, the human soul is exalted above all
egress and regress. It is still, and yet it soareth; it
moveth, and yet it is still. It is, in itself, a testimony that beareth witness to the existence of a
world that is contingent, as well as to the reality
of a world that hath neither beginning nor end.[3]

Bahá'u'lláh

The Birth of the Spirit

O Son of Man! I loved thy creation, hence I
created thee. Wherefore, do thou love Me, that I
may name thy name and fill thy soul with the
spirit of life.[4]

Bahá'u'lláh

Know thou that every soul is fashioned after the

nature of God, each being pure and holy at his birth.[5]

'Abdu'l-Bahá

The soul is not a combination of elements, it is not composed of many atoms, it is of one indivisible substance and therefore eternal. It is entirely out of the order of the physical creation; it is immortal![6]

'Abdu'l-Bahá

... the rational soul, meaning the human spirit, does not descend into the body – that is to say, it does not enter it, for descent and entrance are characteristics of bodies, and the rational soul is exempt from this. The spirit never entered this body ... the spirit is connected with the body, as this light is with this mirror. When the mirror is clear and perfect, the light of the lamp will be apparent in it, and when the mirror becomes covered with dust or breaks, the light will disappear.

The rational soul – that is to say, the human spirit – has neither entered this body nor existed through it ... the rational soul is the substance through which the body exists. The personality of the rational soul is from its beginning ...[7]

'Abdu'l-Bahá

The soul or spirit of the individual comes into

being with the conception of his physical body.[8]

Shoghi Effendi

The Spirit's Birth from This World into the World of God

But the human spirit, unless assisted by the spirit of faith, does not become acquainted with the divine secrets and the heavenly realities. It is like a mirror which, although clear, polished, and brilliant, is still in need of light. Until a ray of the sun reflects upon it, it cannot discover the heavenly secrets.[9]

'Abdu'l-Bahá

Entrance into the Kingdom is through the love of God, through detachment, through holiness and chastity, through truthfulness, purity, stead-fastness, faithfulness and the sacrifice of life.[10]

'Abdu'l-Bahá

. . . unless man is released from the material world, freed from the captivity of materialism and receiving a portion of the bounties of the spiritual world, he shall be deprived of the bestowals and favours of the Kingdom of God . . . But if he is baptized with the Holy Spirit, if he is freed from the bondage of nature, released from animalistic tendencies and advanced in the human realm, he is fitted to enter into the divine Kingdom. The world of the Kingdom is the realm of divine bestowals and the bounties of God. It is attainment of the highest virtues of humanity; it is nearness to God; it is capacity to receive the bounties of the ancient Lord. When man advances to this station, he attains the second birth . . . as long as man is in the matrix of the human world, as long as he is the captive of nature, he is out of touch and without knowledge of the universe of the Kingdom. If he attains rebirth while in the world of nature, he will become informed of the divine world. He will observe that another and a higher world exists. Wonderful bounties descend; eternal life awaits; everlasting glory surrounds him. All the signs of reality and greatness are there. He will see the lights of God. All these experiences will be his when he is born out of the world of nature into the divine world. Therefore, for the perfect man there are two kinds of birth: the first, physical birth, is from the matrix of the mother; the second, or spiritual birth, is from the world of nature. In both he is without knowledge of the new world of existence he is entering. Therefore, rebirth means his release from the captivity of nature, freedom from attachment to this mortal and material life.[11]

'Abdu'l-Bahá

Just as man has been physically born into this world, he may be reborn from the realm and matrix of nature, for the realm of nature is a condition of animalism, darkness and defect. In this second birth he attains the world of the Kingdom. There he witnesses and realizes that the world of nature is a world of gloom, whereas the Kingdom is a world of radiance; the world of nature is a world of defects, the Kingdom is a realm of perfection; the world of nature is a world without enlightenment, the Kingdom of spiritual humanity is a heaven of illumination. Great discoveries and revelations are now possible for him; he has attained the reality of perception; his circle of understanding is illimitably widened; he views the realities of creation, comprehends the divine bounties and unseals the mystery of phenomena. This is the station which Christ has interpreted as the second birth.[12]

'Abdu'l-Bahá

The Inner Life of the Spirit

All praise and glory be to God Who, through the power of His might, hath delivered His creation from the nakedness of non-existence, and clothed it with the mantle of life. From among all created things He hath singled out for His special favour the pure, the gem-like reality of man, and invested it with a unique capacity of knowing Him and of reflecting the greatness of His glory. This twofold distinction conferred upon him hath cleansed away from his heart the rust of every

vain desire, and made him worthy of the vesture
with which his Creator hath deigned to clothe
him. It hath served to rescue his soul from the
wretchedness of ignorance.

This robe with which the body and soul of man
hath been adorned is the very foundation of his
well-being and development. Oh, how blessed the
day when, aided by the grace and might of the
one true God, man will have freed himself from
the bondage and corruption of the world and all
that is therein, and will have attained unto true
and abiding rest beneath the shadow of the Tree
of Knowledge![13]

Bahá'u'lláh

Every soul that walketh humbly with its God, in
this Day, and cleaveth unto Him, shall find itself
invested with the honour and glory of all goodly
names and stations.[14]

Bahá'u'lláh

Having created the world and all that liveth and
moveth therein, He, through the direct operation
of His unconstrained and sovereign Will, chose to
confer upon man the unique distinction and
capacity to know Him and to love Him – a
capacity that must needs be regarded as the
generating impulse and the primary purpose
underlying the whole of creation . . . Upon the
inmost reality of each and every created thing He
hath shed the light of one of His names, and

made it a recipient of the glory of one of His attributes. Upon the reality of man, however, He hath focused the radiance of all of His names and attributes, and made it a mirror of His own Self. Alone of all created things man hath been singled out for so great a favour, so enduring a bounty.[15]

Bahá'u'lláh

The Spirit's Fate after Its Ascension from the Body

And now concerning thy question regarding the soul of man and its survival after death. Know thou of a truth that the soul, after its separation from the body, will continue to progress until it attaineth the presence of God, in a state and condition which neither the revolution of ages and centuries, nor the changes and chances of this world, can alter. It will endure as long as the Kingdom of God, His sovereignty, His dominion and power will endure. It will manifest the signs of God and His attributes, and will reveal His loving kindness and bounty. The movement of My Pen is stilled when it attempteth to befittingly describe the loftiness and glory of so exalted a station. The honour with which the Hand of Mercy will invest the soul is such as no tongue can adequately reveal, nor any other earthly agency describe. Blessed is the soul which, at the hour of its separation from the body, is sanctified from the vain imaginings of the peoples of the world. Such a soul liveth and moveth in accordance with the Will of its Creator, and entereth the all-highest Paradise. The Maids of Heaven, inmates of the loftiest mansions, will circle around it, and the Prophets of God and His chosen ones will seek its companionship. With them that soul will freely converse, and will recount unto them that which it hath been made to endure in the path of God, the Lord of all worlds. If any man be told that which hath been ordained for such a soul in the worlds of God, the Lord of the throne on high and of earth below, his whole being will instantly blaze out in his great longing to attain that most exalted, that sanctified and resplendent station ... The nature of the soul after death can never be described, nor is it meet and permissible to reveal its whole character to the eyes of men. The Prophets and Messengers of God have been sent down for the sole purpose of guiding mankind to the straight Path of Truth. The purpose underlying Their revelation hath been to educate all men, that they may, at the hour of death, ascend, in the utmost purity and sanctity and with absolute detachment, to the throne of the Most High. The light which these souls radiate is responsible for the progress of the world and the advancement of its peoples. They are like unto leaven which leaveneth the world of being, and constitute the animating force through which the arts and wonders of the world are made manifest. Through them the clouds rain their bounty upon men, and the earth

bringeth forth its fruits. All things must needs
have a cause, a motive power, an animating
principle. These souls and symbols of detachment
have provided, and will continue to provide, the
supreme moving impulse in the world of being.
The world beyond is as different from this world
as this world is different from that of the child
while still in the womb of its mother. When the
soul attaineth the Presence of God, it will assume
the form that best befitteth its immortality and is
worthy of its celestial habitation.[16]

Bahá'u'lláh

Thou hast, moreover, asked Me concerning the
state of the soul after its separation from the
body. Know thou, of a truth, that if the soul of
man hath walked in the ways of God, it will,
assuredly, return and be gathered to the glory of
the Beloved. By the righteousness of God! It shall
attain a station such as no pen can depict, or
tongue describe. The soul that hath remained
faithful to the Cause of God, and stood
unwaveringly firm in His Path shall, after his
ascension, be possessed of such power that all the
worlds which the Almighty hath created can
benefit through him. Such a soul provideth, at the
bidding of the Ideal King and Divine Educator,
the pure leaven that leaveneth the world of being,
and furnisheth the power through which the arts
and wonders of the world are made manifest.
Consider how meal needeth leaven to be leavened

with. Those souls that are the symbols of
detachment are the leaven of the world. Meditate
on this, and be of the thankful.[17]

Bahá'u'lláh

As to the soul of man after death, it remains in
the degree of purity to which it has evolved
during life in the physical body, and after it is
freed from the body it remains plunged in the
ocean of God's Mercy.

From the moment the soul leaves the body and
arrives in the Heavenly World, its evolution is
spiritual, and that evolution is: The approaching
unto God.[18]

'Abdu'l-Bahá

The progress of man's spirit in the divine world,
after the severance of its connection with the
body of dust, is through the bounty and grace of
the Lord alone, or through the intercession and
the sincere prayers of other human souls, or
through the charities and important good works
which are performed in its name.[19]

'Abdu'l-Bahá

8
Themes for Meditation

In its Riḍván message of 1967 the Universal House of Justice identified a number of themes which Baháʼís were encouraged to pursue to deepen their understanding of their religion:

> What is Baháʼuʼlláh's purpose for the human race? For what ends did He submit to the appalling cruelties and indignities heaped upon Him? What does He mean by a 'new race of men'? What are the profound changes which He will bring about? The answers are to be found in the Sacred Writings of our Faith and in their interpretation by ʻAbduʼl-Bahá and our beloved Guardian. Let the friends immerse themselves in this ocean . . .[1]

Meditation on these themes, using the Baháʼí sacred writings, will, it is suggested, provide a 'clearer apprehension of the purpose of God for man' and identify 'the objectives for which the

Báb gave His life, Bahá'u'lláh endured such suf-
ferings as none before Him had ever endured, the
Master and after Him the Guardian bore their
trials and afflictions with such superhuman forti-
tude'.[2] Some examples of the answers to these
questions that can be found in the Bahá'í teachings are provided here.

What is Bahá'u'lláh's purpose for the human race?

The Purpose of the one true God, exalted be His
glory, in revealing Himself unto men is to lay bare
those gems that lie hidden within the mine of
their true and inmost selves.[3]

Bahá'u'lláh

The purpose of the one true God in manifesting
Himself is to summon all mankind to truthfulness
and sincerity, to piety and trustworthiness, to
resignation and submissiveness to the Will of God,
to forbearance and kindliness, to uprightness and
wisdom. His object is to array every man with the
mantle of a saintly character, and to adorn him
with the ornament of holy and goodly deeds.[4]

Bahá'u'lláh

This Wronged One, rid of all attachment to the
world, hath striven with utmost endeavour to
quench the fire of animosity and hatred which
burneth fiercely in the hearts of the peoples of the

earth. It behoveth every just and fair-minded person to render thanks unto God – exalted be His glory – and to arise to promote this pre-eminent Cause, that fire may turn into light, and hatred may give way to fellowship and love. I swear by the righteousness of God! This is the sole purpose of this Wronged One.[5]

Bahá'u'lláh

The fundamental purpose animating the Faith of God and His Religion is to safeguard the interests and promote the unity of the human race, and to foster the spirit of love and fellowship amongst men.[6]

Bahá'u'lláh

. . . the purpose of the Manifestation of God and the dawning of the limitless lights of the Invisible is to educate the souls of men, and refine the character of every living man – so that blessed individuals, who have freed themselves from the murk of the animal world, shall rise up with those qualities which are the adornings of the reality of man. The purpose is that earthlings should turn into the people of Heaven, and those who walk in darkness should come into the light, and those who are excluded should join the inner circle of the Kingdom, and those who are as nothing should become intimates of the everlasting Glory. It is that the portionless should gain their share of the boundless sea, and the ignorant drink their fill from the living fount of knowledge; that those who thirst for blood should forsake their savagery, and those who are barbed of claw should turn gentle and forbearing, and those who love war should seek instead for true conciliation; it is that the brutal, their talons razor-sharp, should enjoy the benefits of lasting peace; that the foul should learn that there is a realm of purity, and the tainted find their way to the rivers of holiness.[7]

'Abdu'l-Bahá

For what ends did Bahá'u'lláh submit to the appalling cruelties and indignities heaped upon Him?

The Ancient Beauty hath consented to be bound with chains that mankind may be released from its bondage, and hath accepted to be made a prisoner within this most mighty Stronghold that the whole world may attain unto true liberty. He hath drained to its dregs the cup of sorrow, that all the peoples of the earth may attain unto abiding joy, and be filled with gladness. This is of the mercy of your Lord, the Compassionate, the Most Merciful. We have accepted to be abased, O believers in the Unity of God, that ye may be exalted, and have suffered manifold afflictions, that ye might prosper and flourish. He Who hath come to build anew the whole world, behold, how they that have joined partners with God have forced Him to dwell within the most desolate of cities![8]

Bahá'u'lláh

We have accepted to be tried by ills and troubles, that ye may sanctify yourselves from all earthly defilements. Why, then, refuse ye to ponder Our purpose in your hearts? By the righteousness of God! Whoso will reflect upon the tribulations We have suffered, his soul will assuredly melt away with sorrow. Thy Lord Himself beareth witness to the truth of My words. We have sustained the weight of all calamities to sanctify you from all earthly corruption, and ye are yet indifferent.[9]

Bahá'u'lláh

He bore all these ordeals and catastrophes and difficulties in order that, in the world of humanity, a selflessness might become apparent.

In order that the Most Great Peace might become a reality in the world of humanity.

In order that waiting souls might become manifest as the very angels of Heaven.

In order that Heavenly miracles might become perfected among men.

In order that the priceless, precious bestowal of God in the human temple, the Mind of humanity, might develop to its fullest capacity.

In order that infants may be (in truth) likenesses of God, even as it has been written in the Bible: 'We shall create men in Our Own Image.'

Bahá'u'lláh bore all these ordeals and catastrophes for this:

That our hearts might be illumined.

That our spirits might become glad.

That our imperfections might be replaced by virtues.

That our ignorance might be transformed into knowledge.

In order that we might acquire the fruits of humanity and obtain Heavenly graces.

Although we are now on earth, let us walk [travel] in the Kingdom.

Although we are needy, let us plead for Heavenly treasure.

For these bounties to us has the Blessed Perfection borne so great difficulties.[10]

'Abdu'l-Bahá

What does Bahá'u'lláh mean by a 'new race of men'?

A race of men, incomparable in character, shall be raised up which, with the feet of detachment, will tread under all who are in heaven and on earth, and will cast the sleeve of holiness over all that hath been created from water and clay.[11]

Bahá'u'lláh

There lay concealed within the Holy Veil, and prepared for the service of God, a company of His chosen ones who shall be manifested unto men, who shall aid His Cause, who shall be afraid of no one, though the entire human race rise up and war against them. These are the ones who, before the gaze of the dwellers on earth and the denizens of heaven, shall arise and, shouting aloud, acclaim the name of the Almighty, and summon the children of men to the path of God, the All-Glorious, the All-Praised.[12]

Bahá'u'lláh

And yet, is not the object of every Revelation to effect a transformation in the whole character of mankind, a transformation that shall manifest itself both outwardly and inwardly, that shall affect both its inner life and external conditions? For if the character of mankind be not changed, the futility of God's universal Manifestations would be apparent.[13]

Bahá'u'lláh

You are the bearers of the name of God in this Day. You have been chosen as the repositories of His mystery. It behoves each one of you to manifest the attributes of God, and to exemplify by your deeds and words the signs of His righteousness, His power and glory. The very members of your body must bear witness to the loftiness of your purpose, the integrity of your life, the reality of your faith, and the exalted character of your devotion.[14]

The Báb

. . . ye must conduct yourselves in such a manner that ye may stand out distinguished and brilliant as the sun among other souls. Should any one of you enter a city, he should become a centre of attraction by reason of his sincerity, his faithfulness and love, his honesty and fidelity, his truthfulness and loving-kindness towards all the peoples of the world . . . [15]

'Abdu'l-Bahá

What are the profound changes which Bahá'u'lláh will bring about?

Let there be no mistake. The principle of the Oneness of Mankind – the pivot round which all the teachings of Bahá'u'lláh revolve – is no mere outburst of ignorant emotionalism or an expression of vague and pious hope. Its appeal is not to be merely identified with a reawakening of the spirit of brotherhood and good-will among men, nor does it aim solely at the fostering of harmonious cooperation among individual peoples and nations. Its implications are deeper, its claims greater than any which the Prophets of old were allowed to advance. Its message is applicable not only to the individual, but concerns itself primarily with the nature of those essential relationships that must bind all the states and nations as members of one human family. It does not constitute merely the enunciation of an ideal, but stands inseparably associated with an institution adequate to embody its truth, demonstrate its validity, and perpetuate its influence. It implies an organic change in the structure of present-day society, a change such as the world has not yet experienced. It constitutes a challenge, at once bold and universal, to outworn shibboleths of national creeds – creeds that have had their day and which must, in the ordinary course of events as shaped and controlled by Providence, give way to a new gospel, fundamentally different from, and infinitely superior to, what the world has already conceived. It calls for no less than the reconstruction and the demilitarization of the whole civilized world – a world organically unified in all the essential aspects of its life, its political machinery, its spiritual aspiration, its trade and finance, its script and language, and yet infinite in the diversity of the national characteristics of its federated units.

It represents the consummation of human evolution – an evolution that has had its earliest beginnings in the birth of family life, its subsequent development in the achievement of tribal solidarity, leading in turn to the constitution of the city-state, and expanding later into the institution of independent and sovereign nations.

The principle of the Oneness of Mankind, as proclaimed by Bahá'u'lláh, carries with it no more and no less than a solemn assertion that

attainment to this final stage in this stupendous
evolution is not only necessary but inevitable,
that its realization is fast approaching, and that
nothing short of a power that is born of God can
succeed in establishing it.[16]

Shoghi Effendi

The unity of the human race, as envisaged by
Bahá'u'lláh, implies the establishment of a world
commonwealth in which all nations, races, creeds
and classes are closely and permanently united,
and in which the autonomy of its state members
and the personal freedom and initiative of the
individuals that compose them are definitely and
completely safeguarded. This commonwealth
must, as far as we can visualize it, consist of a
world legislature, whose members will, as the
trustees of the whole of mankind, ultimately
control the entire resources of all the component
nations, and will enact such laws as shall be
required to regulate the life, satisfy the needs and
adjust the relationships of all races and peoples.
A world executive, backed by an international
Force, will carry out the decisions arrived at, and
apply the laws enacted by, this world legislature,
and will safeguard the organic unity of the whole
commonwealth. A world tribunal will adjudicate
and deliver its compulsory and final verdict in all
and any disputes that may arise between the
various elements constituting this universal
system. A mechanism of world inter-

communication will be devised, embracing the whole planet, freed from national hindrances and restrictions, and functioning with marvellous swiftness and perfect regularity. A world metropolis will act as the nerve centre of a world civilization, the focus towards which the unifying forces of life will converge and from which its energizing influences will radiate. A world language will either be invented or chosen from among the existing languages and will be taught in the schools of all the federated nations as an auxiliary to their mother tongue. A world script, a world literature, a uniform and universal system of currency, of weights and measures, will simplify and facilitate intercourse and understanding among the nations and races of mankind. In such a world society, science and religion, the two most potent forces in human life, will be reconciled, will cooperate, and will harmoniously develop. The press will, under such a system, while giving full scope to the expression of the diversified views and convictions of mankind, cease to be mischievously manipulated by vested interests, whether private or public, and will be liberated from the influence of contending governments and peoples. The economic resources of the world will be organized, its sources of raw materials will be tapped and fully utilized, its markets will be coordinated and developed, and the distribution of its products will be equitably regulated.

National rivalries, hatred, and intrigues will cease, and racial animosity and prejudice will be replaced by racial amity, understanding and cooperation. The causes of religious strife will be permanently removed, economic barriers and restrictions will be completely abolished, and the inordinate distinction between classes will be obliterated. Destitution on the one hand, and gross accumulation of ownership on the other, will disappear. The enormous energy dissipated and wasted on war, whether economic or political, will be consecrated to such ends as will extend the range of human inventions and technical development, to the increase of the productivity of mankind, to the extermination of disease, to the extension of scientific research, to the raising of the standard of physical health, to the sharpening and refinement of the human brain, to the exploitation of the unused and unsuspected resources of the planet, to the prolongation of human life, and to the furtherance of any other agency that can stimulate the intellectual, the moral, and spiritual life of the entire human race.

A world federal system, ruling the whole earth and exercising unchallengeable authority over its unimaginably vast resources, blending and embodying the ideals of both the East and the West, liberated from the curse of war and its miseries, and bent on the exploitation of all the available sources of energy on the surface of the planet, a system in which Force is made the servant of Justice, whose life is sustained by its universal recognition of one God and by its allegiance to one common Revelation – such is the goal towards which humanity, impelled by the unifying forces of life, is moving.[17]

Shoghi Effendi

Bibliography

'Abdu'l-Bahá. *Foundations of World Unity*. Wilmette, Illinois: Bahá'í Publishing Trust, 1971.

—— *Paris Talks*. London: Bahá'í Publishing Trust, 1979.

—— *The Promulgation of Universal Peace*. Wilmette, Illinois: Bahá'í Publishing Trust, 1982.

—— *Selections from the Writings of 'Abdu'l-Bahá*. Haifa: Bahá'í World Centre, 1978.

—— *Some Answered Questions*. Wilmette, Illinois: Bahá'í Publishing Trust, 1990.

—— *Tablets of Abdu'l-Baha Abbas*. New York: Baha'i Publishing Committee, 1930.

Bahá'í Prayers. Wilmette, Illinois: Bahá'í Publishing Trust, 1991.

Bahá'í World Faith. Wilmette, Illinois: Bahá'í Publishing Trust, 1971.

Bahá'u'lláh. *Epistle to the Son of the Wolf*. Wilmette, Illinois: Bahá'í Publishing Trust, 1988.

—— *Gleanings from the Writings of Bahá'u'lláh*. Wilmette, Illinois: Bahá'í Publishing Trust, 1983.

—— *The Hidden Words*. Wilmette, Illinois: Bahá'í Publishing Trust, 1990.

—— The Kitáb-i-Aqdas. Haifa: Bahá'í World Centre, 1992.

—— The Kitáb-i-Íqán. Wilmette, Illinois: Bahá'í Publishing Trust, 1989.

—— Prayers and Meditations. Wilmette, Illinois: Bahá'í Publishing Trust, 1962.

—— The Seven Valleys and the Four Valleys. Wilmette, Illinois: Bahá'í Publishing Trust, 1991.

—— Tablets of Bahá'u'lláh revealed after the Kitáb-i-Aqdas. Wilmette, Illinois: Bahá'í Publishing Trust, 1988.

Blomfield, Lady. The Chosen Highway. Wilmette, Illinois: Bahá'í Publishing Trust, 1967.

The Compilation of Compilations. Victoria, Australia: Bahá'í Publications Australia, 1991.

Hewitt, James. The Complete Yoga Book. London: Rider, 1991.

Lights of Guidance: A Bahá'í Reference File. Compiled by Helen Hornby. New Delhi: Bahá'í Publishing Trust, 2nd edn. 1988.

Maxwell, May. An Early Pilgrimage. Oxford: George Ronald, 1976.

Nabíl. The Dawn-Breakers. Wilmette, Illinois: Bahá'í Publishing Trust, 1962.

Nicholson, Reynold A. The Mystics of Islam. London: Routledge and Kegan Paul, 1979.

Russell, Peter. The TM Technique. London: Routledge and Kegan Paul, 1978.

Scholl, Steven. 'The Remembrance of God: A Sufi invocation technique in Bábí and Bahá'í scriptures', manuscript.

Scott, David and Tony Doubleday. The Elements of Zen. Shaftesbury, Dorset: Element, 1992.

Shah, Idries. *Sufi Thought and Action*. London: The Octagon Press, 1993.

Shoghi Effendi. *The Advent of Divine Justice*. Wilmette, Illinois: Bahá'í Publishing Trust, 1990.

—— *God Passes By. Wilmette*, Illinois: Bahá'í Publishing Trust, 1970.

—— *High Endeavors: Messages to Alaska*. Anchorage, Alaska: National Spiritual Assembly of the Bahá'ís of Alaska, 1976.

—— *The World Order of Bahá'u'lláh*. Wilmette, Illinois: Bahá'í Publishing Trust, 1991.

The Universal House of Justice. *Wellspring of Guidance*. Wilmette, Illinois: Bahá'í Publishing Trust, 1969.

Notes & References

Preface

1. From a letter written on behalf of Shoghi Effendi to an individual believer, 4 February 1950. *Compilation*, vol. 2, no. 1973, p. 315.

Chapter 1: Beginnings

1. Bahá'u'lláh, *Kitáb-i-Íqán*, p. 238.

2. Letter of the Universal House of Justice to a European National Spiritual Assembly, 1 September 1983.

3. Shoghi Effendi, *Directives from the Guardian*, p. 27.

4. From a letter written on behalf of Shoghi Effendi to an individual believer, 20 November 1937, *Lights of Guidance*, no. 1518, p. 463.

5. Letter of the Universal House of Justice to a European National Spiritual Assembly, 1 September 1983. *Lights of Guidance*, no. 1836, p. 541.

6. ibid.

7. Letter from Shoghi Effendi to an individual believer, 8 December 1935, *Lights of Guidance*, no. 1845, p. 543.

8. 'Abdu'l-Bahá, *Paris Talks*, p. 175.

9. Letter of the Universal House of Justice to a European National Spiritual Assembly, 1 September 1983, *Lights of Guidance*, no. 1837, p. 541.

10. From a letter written on behalf of Shoghi Effendi to an individual believer, 19 November 1945. *Lights of Guidance*, no. 1519, p. 463.

11. Letter written on behalf of Shoghi Effendi to an individual believer, 6 December 1935. *Compilation*, vol. 2, no, 1761, p. 237.

Chapter 2: What is Meditation?

1. Bahá'u'lláh, *Kitáb-i-Íqán*, p. 8.

2. The text of this talk can be found in *Paris Talks*, pp. 173–6. All the quotations in this chapter are taken from this talk unless otherwise indicated.

3. 'Abdu'l-Bahá, *Selections*, p. 41.

Chapter 3: Meditation Techniques

1. Letter from Shoghi Effendi to an individual believer, 8 December 1935, *Lights of Guidance*, no. 1845, p. 543.

2. Shah, *Sufi Thought and Action*, p. 1.

3. ibid.

4. ibid. p. 2.

5. Scholl, 'The Remembrance of God', p. 2.

6. ibid. p. 7.

7. Gardet, quoted in Scholl, ibid. pp. 5–6.

8. ibid. p. 5.

9. Nicholson, *Mystics of Islam*, p. 46.

10. ibid. p. 47.

11. ibid.

12. ibid.

13. Scholl, 'The Remembrance of God', p. 15.

14. Russell, *TM Technique*, p. 15.

15. ibid. p. 48.

16. ibid. p. 61.

17. ibid. p. 50.

18. Hewitt, *Complete Yoga Book*, p. 3.

19. ibid. p. 371.

20. ibid. p. 377.

21. ibid. p. 397.

22. ibid. p. 399.

23. ibid. p. 421.

24. ibid, p. 427.

25. ibid. p. 430.

26. ibid. p. 431.

27. ibid. p. 439.

28. ibid.

29. ibid. p. 442.

30. Scott and Doubleday, *Elements of Zen*, p. 2.

31. ibid. p. 3.

32. ibid. p. 4.

33. ibid. p. 44.

34. Cited in ibid. p. 61.

35. Bahá'u'lláh, *Gleanings*, p. 262.

36. ibid. pp. 65–7.

37. Bahá'u'lláh, Kitáb-i-Aqdas, para. 18.

38. Bahá'u'lláh, *Tablets*. p. 155.

39. Bahá'u'lláh, *Gleanings*, p. 138.

40. ibid. p. 275.

41. ibid. pp. 294–5.

42. Quoted in Shoghi Effendi, *God Passes By*, p. 119.

43. Bahá'u'lláh, *Prayers and Meditations*, pp. 82–3.

44. Bahá'u'lláh, *Hidden Words*, Arabic no. 13.

45. ibid. Arabic no. 7.

46. ibid. Arabic no. 12.

47. ibid. Arabic no. 11.

48. Bahá'u'lláh, *Gleanings*, p. 70.

49. Bahá'u'lláh, *Tablets*, p. 17.

50. Bahá'u'lláh, *Epistle*, p. 115.

51. Bahá'u'lláh, *Prayers and Meditations*, pp. 194–5.

52. Gardet, quoted by Scholl, 'The Remembrance of God', p. 9.

53. Bahá'u'lláh, Kitáb-i-Aqdas, para. 149.

54. Bahá'u'lláh, Kitáb-i-Aqdas, para. 116.

55. Bahá'u'lláh, *Hidden Words*, Arabic no. 16.

56. Bahá'u'lláh, *Prayers and Meditations*, p. 139.

57. Bahá'u'lláh, *Tablets*, p. 17.

58. Bahá'u'lláh, *Prayers and Meditations*, p. 174.

59. ibid. p. 221.

60. 'Abdu'l-Bahá, *Paris Talks*, p. 61.

61. Bahá'u'lláh, *Hidden Words*, Arabic no. 13.

62. Bahá'u'lláh, *Tablets*, p. 96.

63. 'Abdu'l-Bahá, *Bahá'í World Faith*, p. 384.

64. Bahá'u'lláh, *Prayers and Meditations*, p. 161.

65. ibid. p. 214.

66. Bahá'u'lláh, *Hidden Words*, Persian no. 70.

67. Bahá'u'lláh, *Gleanings*, pp. 325–6.

68. Bahá'u'lláh, *Prayers and Meditations*, p. 89.

69. Robert Gulick, Preface to Bahá'u'lláh, *Seven Valleys*, p. xi.

70. Bahá'u'lláh, *Seven Valleys*, pp. 35–6.

71. Bahá'u'lláh, *Hidden Words*, Arabic no. 31.

72. Bahá'u'lláh, Kitáb-i-Aqdas, para. 18.

73. ibid. question 81.

74. ibid. question 58.

75. ibid. note 22.

76. ibid. note 4.

77. Scholl, 'The Remembrance of God', p. 34.

78. Bahá'u'lláh, *Gleanings*, p. 11.

79. From a letter written on behalf of Shoghi Effendi to an individual believer, *Lights of Guidance*, no. 1493, p. 458.

80. From a letter written on behalf of the Universal House of Justice to a European National Spiritual Assembly, 1 September 1983.

81. ibid.

82. Bahá'u'lláh, Kitáb-i-Aqdas, p. 95.

83. Bahá'u'lláh, in *Bahá'í Prayers*, p. 221.

84. Bahá'u'lláh, *Prayers and Meditations*, p. 288.

85. Bahá'u'lláh, in Bahá'í Prayers, p. 91.

86. Bahá'u'lláh, Kitáb-i-Aqdas, pp. 101–2.

87. 'Abdu'l-Bahá, 'Table Talk', in *Lights of Guidance*, no. 1370, p. 412–13.

88. Bahá'u'lláh, Kitáb-i-Aqdas, para. 51.

89. 'Abdu'l-Bahá in *Bahá'í World Faith*, p. 378.

90. From a letter written on behalf of Shoghi Effendi, *Lights of Guidance*, no. 823, pp. 245–6.

91. From a letter written on behalf of Shoghi Effendi to an individual believer, 19 November 1945. *Lights of Guidance*, no. 1519, p. 463.

Chapter 4: Short Verses for Meditation

1. Bahá'u'lláh, *Seven Valleys*, p. 28.

2. Bahá'u'lláh, *Hidden Words*, Persian no. 3.
3. 'Abdu'l-Bahá, *Promulgation*, p. 337.
4. 'Abdu'l-Bahá, *Selections*, p. 3.
5. ibid. p. 27.
6. ibid.
7. ibid.
8. ibid.
9. ibid.
10. 'Abdu'l-Bahá, *Paris Talks*, p. 125.
11. 'Abdu'l-Bahá, *Promulgation*, p. 15.
12. 'Abdu'l-Bahá, *Selections*, p. 66.
13. 'Abdu'l-Bahá, *Promulgation*, p. 15.
14. 'Abdu'l-Bahá, *Paris Talks*, p. 36.
15. ibid. p. 179.
16. ibid.
17. ibid.
18. ibid.
19. ibid.
20. 'Abdu'l-Bahá, *Selections*, p. 203.
21. Attributed to 'Abdu'l-Bahá.
22. Bahá'u'lláh, *Gleanings*, p. 288.
23. Bahá'u'lláh *Tablets*, p. 27.
24. ibid. p. 67.
25. Bahá'u'lláh, *Hidden Words*, Arabic no. 68.
26. Bahá'u'lláh, *Kitáb-i-Íqán*, p. 159.
27. 'Abdu'l-Bahá, *Paris Talks*, p. 128.
28. ibid. p. 136.
29. 'Abdu'l-Bahá, *Promulgation*, p. 151.
30. ibid. p. 126.
31. Bahá'u'lláh, *Kitáb-i-Íqán*, p. 120.
32. 'Abdu'l-Bahá, *Selections*, p. 177.

33. 'Abdu'l-Bahá, *Foundations*, p. 78.

34. Bahá'u'lláh, *Gleanings*, p. 286.

35. Bahá'u'lláh, *Tablets*, p. 37.

36. Bahá'u'lláh, *Epistle*, p. 28.

37. 'Abdu'l-Bahá, *Paris Talks*, p. 15.

38. 'Abdu'l-Bahá, *Bahá'í World Faith*, p. 231.

39. Bahá'u'lláh, *Hidden Words*, Arabic no. 13.

40. Bahá'u'lláh, *Tablets*, pp. 169–79.

41. 'Abdu'l-Bahá, *Some Answered Questions*, p. 300.

42. 'Abdu'l-Bahá, *Bahá'í World Faith*, p. 227.

43. ibid.

44. 'Abdu'l-Bahá, *Selections*, p. 192.

45. 'Abdu'l-Bahá, *Tablets*, p. 558.

46. 'Abdu'l-Bahá, *Paris Talks*, p. 111.

47. 'Abdu'l-Bahá, quoted in Blomfield, *Chosen Highway*, p. 166.

48. ibid.

49. Bahá'u'lláh, *Gleanings*, p. 185.

50. ibid.

51. 'Abdu'l-Bahá, *Paris Talks*, p. 15.

52. Bahá'u'lláh, *Gleanings*, p. 196.

53. ibid.

54. ibid.

55. Bahá'u'lláh, *Tablets*, p. 138.

56. ibid. p. 156.

57. ibid.

58. Bahá'u'lláh, *Prayers and Meditations*, p. 313.

59. Bahá'u'lláh, *Gleanings*, p. 70.

60. 'Abdu'l-Bahá, *Promulgation*, p. 4.

61. ibid.

62. Bahá'u'lláh, *Gleanings*, p. 158.

63. ibid. p. 161.

64. Bahá'u'lláh, quoted in Shoghi Effendi, *Advent*, p. 24.

65. Bahá'u'lláh, *Epistle*, p. 15.

66. Bahá'u'lláh, *Prayers and Meditations*, p. 11.

67. 'Abdu'l-Bahá, *Tablets*, p. 214.

68. ibid.

69. 'Abdu'l-Bahá, *Promulgation*, p. 148.

70. 'Abdu'l-Bahá, *Tablets*, p. 553.

71. 'Abdu'l-Bahá, *Selections*, p. 245.

72. ibid. p. 65.

73. ibid. p. 76.

74. 'Abdu'l-Bahá, *Tablets*, p. 65.

75. Bahá'u'lláh, *Tablets*, p. 138.

76. 'Abdu'l-Bahá, *Paris Talks*, p. 171.

77. 'Abdu'l-Bahá, *Tablets*, p. 477.

78. Bahá'u'lláh, *Epistle*, p. 17.

79. 'Abdu'l-Bahá, *Paris Talks*, p. 50.

80. ibid. p. 51.

81. ibid. p. 50.

82. 'Abdu'l-Bahá, *Paris Talks*, p. 29.

83. ibid. p. 169.

84. 'Abdu'l-Bahá, *Tablets*, p. 10.

85. 'Abdu'l-Bahá, *Paris Talks*, p. 108.

86. ibid. p. 58.

87. ibid. p. 51.

88. 'Abdu'l-Bahá, *Tablets*, p. 641.

Chapter 5: Longer Meditations

1. Bahá'u'lláh, *Prayers and Meditations*, pp. 192–6.

2. ibid. pp. 87–94.

5. ibid. p. 106–10.

Chapter 6: 'Ponder This in Thy Heart'

1. Bahá'u'lláh, *Prayers and Meditations*, p. 304.

2. Bahá'u'lláh, *Seven Valleys*, pp. 1–2.

3. Bahá'u'lláh, *Prayers and Meditations*, p. 55.

4. ibid. p. 126.

5. Bahá'u'lláh, *Epistle*, p. 9.

6. Bahá'u'lláh, *Kitáb-i-Íqán*, p. 167.

7. Bahá'u'lláh, *Epistle*, pp. 75–6.

8. ibid. p. 110.

9. Bahá'u'lláh, *Kitáb-i-Íqán*, p. 47.

10. ibid. p. 70.

11. Bahá'u'lláh, *Hidden Words*, Persian no. 26.

12. ibid. Arabic no. 46.

13. Bahá'u'lláh, *Gleanings*, pp. 74–5.

14. Bahá'u'lláh, *Epistle*, p. 12.

15. Bahá'u'lláh, *Gleanings*, pp. 143–4.

16. ibid. p. 325.

17. Bahá'u'lláh, *Kitáb-i-Íqán*, pp. 16–17.

18. Bahá'u'lláh, *Gleanings*, p. 124.

19. ibid. pp. 119–20.

20. ibid. pp. 160–1.

21. ibid. p. 162.

22. ibid. pp. 151–3.

23. ibid. pp. 157–8.

24. ibid.

25. Bahá'u'lláh, *Hidden Words*, Arabic no. 68.

26. ibid. Arabic no. 2.

27. Bahá'u'lláh, *Gleanings*, p. 9.

Chapter 7: 'Great Questions'

1. 'Abdu'l-Bahá, *Paris Talks*, p. 174.
2. Bahá'u'lláh, *Gleanings*, p. 158–9.
3. ibid. pp. 161–2.
4. Bahá'u'lláh, *Hidden Words*, Arabic no. 4.
5. 'Abdu'l-Bahá, *Selections*, p. 190.
6. 'Abdu'l-Bahá, *Paris Talks,* p. 91.
7. 'Abdu'l-Bahá, *Some Answered Questions*, pp. 239–40.
8. From a letter written on behalf of Shoghi Effendi, *High Endeavors*, p. 69.
9. 'Abdu'l-Bahá, in *Bahá'í World Faith*, p. 317.
10. 'Abdu'l-Bahá, *Some Answered Questions*, p. 242.
11. 'Abdu'l-Bahá, *Promulgation*, pp. 304–5.
12. ibid. pp. 332.
13. Bahá'u'lláh, *Gleanings*, pp. 77–8.
14. ibid. p. 159.
15. ibid. p. 65.
16. Bahá'u'lláh, *Gleanings*, pp. 155–7.
17. ibid. p. 161.
18. 'Abdu'l-Bahá, *Paris Talks*, p. 66.
19. 'Abdu'l-Bahá, *Some Answered Questions*, p. 240.

Chapter 8: Themes for Meditation

1. From the Message of the Universal House of Justice to the Bahá'ís of the World, Riḍván 1967, *Wellspring of Guidance*, p. 114.
2. ibid. pp. 113–14.
3. Bahá'u'lláh, *Gleanings*, p. 287.
4. ibid. p. 299.
5. Bahá'u'lláh, *Tablets*, p. 44.

6. Bahá'u'lláh, *Gleanings*, p. 215.

7. 'Abdu'l-Bahá, *Selections*, pp. 10–11.

8. Bahá'u'lláh, *Gleanings*, pp. 99–100.

9. ibid. p. 307.

10. 'Abdu'l-Bahá, quoted in Blomfield, *Chosen Highway*, pp. 258–9.

11. Bahá'u'lláh, quoted in Shoghi Effendi, *Advent of Divine Justice*, p. 31.

12. Bahá'u'lláh, *Gleanings*, pp. 280–1.

13. Bahá'u'lláh, *Kitáb-i-Íqán*, pp. 240–1.

14. The Báb, quoted in Nabíl, *Dawn-Breakers*, p. 92.

15. 'Abdu'l-Bahá, *Selections*, p. 71.

16. Shoghi Effendi, *World Order*, pp. 42–3.

17. ibid. pp. 203–4.